THE *Last Week*

ATONEMENT
AND RESURRECTION

BARRETT A. SLADE

CFI
An imprint of Cedar Fort, Inc.
Springville, Utah

ISBN 13: 978-1-4621-3698-8

Published by CFI, an imprint of Cedar Fort, Inc.
2373 W. 700 S., Springville, UT 84663
Distributed by Cedar Fort, Inc., www.cedarfort.com

Library of Congress Control Number: 2020930832

Cover design by Shawnda T. Craig
Cover design © 2020 Cedar Fort, Inc.

Printed in the United States of America

10 9 8 7 6 5 4 3 2 1

Printed on acid-free paper

To Patty, the love of my life.

To Cami, Tanner, and Kelli,
the most precious gifts of my life.

CONTENTS

PREFACE

As the Easter season approached in the spring of 2018, I wanted to study the last week of the Savior's mortal ministry. So, I sought after a book that focused on that. I had three criteria: 1) it shouldn't be lengthy and should include a nice summary of the Savior's last week; 2) it needed to contain the actual scriptural account; and 3) it would focus primarily on material from the scriptures of The Church of Jesus Christ of Latter-day Saints, including the Bible Dictionary. It seemed that everything I came across was too long because it included His entire ministry, did not contain the scriptural account, or did not focus on the scriptures of the Church. I decided to write the book myself.

My objective was not to provide a comprehensive scholarly reference book on the life of Christ, for there are many wonderful New Testament commentaries that do just that. My objective was to provide a basic scriptural account and summary of the Savior's last week on earth.

With that in mind, I used the framework provided in the LDS edition of the King James Bible titled Harmony of the Gospels, Section IV, The Last Week: Atonement and Resurrection (see page 769).[1] This section has 102 subsections that provide a chronological outline of the last week of the Lord's mortal ministry.

Using this outline, I first provide the reader with a summary of the forthcoming scriptural verses and then the actual Gospel account. When the Gospel author quotes an individual, I have identified the speaker in brackets and bolded the text. In some cases, I have included supporting references found in the Bible Dictionary and related passages from the Joseph Smith Translation of the New Testament. In rare cases, I have also included references to other sources not found in the scriptures.

As you read and study the Savior's last week of His mortal sojourn, I pray that you may experience a renewal of spirit, develop a deeper love and appreciation for the Savior of the world, and come to know as I do that Jesus is the Christ.

FOREWORD

The final week of the Savior's mortal ministry, combined with His glorious Resurrection from the dead, provide a magnificent finale for His eternal Atonement for all of Heavenly Father's children. In this book, Barrett Slade provides the reader with a powerful, concise, and spiritual account and study, based in the scriptures, of the events and details of the culminating week wherein the Only Begotten Son of God fulfilled the Father's will.

There is power in the scriptures themselves, and Brother Slade has done a great work in bringing them to the forefront, in proper order, chronicling the Savior's final week in mortality and His Resurrection. The format is delightfully simple and makes a pleasant read: First, a brief summary of the event or topic in chronological order, with commentary about what happened at that point in the final week of the Master's ministry, followed by the actual verses of scripture referring to that event.

With this simple format, Brother Slade makes these passages of scripture come to life for you by first telling you what you are going to read and then having you read it in the scriptures themselves. This lends extra understanding and opportunity for the Holy Ghost to be your Teacher.

The notes at the end of the book offer a wealth of additional insights into Jewish culture and practice that add rich meaning and understanding for the reader.

In summary, this book will prove to be an extremely valuable contribution to the knowledge base and testimony of all who read and study it. I highly recommend it.

—David J. Ridges

1

TO JERUSALEM FOR PASSOVER

JOHN 11:55–57
Location: Jerusalem Region

Summary

Approximately three years after the beginning of His ministry and a week before the Feast of the Passover,[2] the Lord traveled to Jerusalem[3] for this purification[4] event, an important tradition of the people. The chief priests and Pharisees[5] expected the Savior to go to Jerusalem to participate in this event, and it was at this time while in the temple[6] that they began to conspire on how they might "take" Him. Luke 11 provides some insight into the reason they hated Him and sought to take His life. The Lord was quite bold in telling the Pharisees that they were hypocrites because of their strict obedience to outward "ceremonial rules" but inward were not pure in heart. They were very prideful and offended by the word of the Lord. This led to great hatred and resentment toward Him; therefore, they sought ways to "catch something out of his mouth, that they might accuse him" (Luke 11:53–54).

> **JOHN 11:55–57**
> 55 And the Jews' passover was nigh at hand: and many went out of the country up to Jerusalem before the passover, to purify themselves.

1

56 Then sought they for Jesus, and spake among themselves, as they stood in the temple, What think ye, that he will not come to the feast?

57 Now both the chief priests and the Pharisees had given a commandment, that, if any man knew where he were, he should shew it, that they might take him.

2

THE SIXTH DAY
BEFORE PASSOVER

JOHN 12:1
Location: Bethany

Summary

Six days before the Passover feast, the Savior went to Bethany,[7] where Lazarus[8] was raised from the dead.

JOHN 12:1

1 Then Jesus six days before the passover came to Bethany, where Lazarus was which had been dead, whom he raised from the dead.

3

MARY ANOINTS JESUS

MATTHEW 26:6–13; MARK 14:3–9;
JOHN 12:2–8
Location: Bethany

Summary

Six days prior to the Passover feast, the Lord arrived in Bethany (about two miles east of Jerusalem) to the house of Simon the leper,[9] who was the brother of Lazarus, Martha, and Mary. These were close friends and associates of the Lord. As He sat eating meat (or dinner), Mary[10] poured spikenard[11] from an alabaster box[12] on the Lord's head and feet and rubbed His feet with her hair. This ointment was a very precious oil that was worth three hundred pence, the equivalent to a man's wages for one year,[13] and was generally only used on very sacred occasions, such as burial.[14] Some of the disciples, including the Apostle Judas Iscariot,[15] complained that Mary's actions were inappropriate, but the Lord rebuked them. This experience teaches us two fundamental principles: 1) some things are more important than others;[16] and 2) having divine discernment is essential in understanding the difference.

In this case, Mary, the sister of Lazarus and Martha, was sensitive to the Spirit. She knew that Jesus was the Savior and that He would soon fulfill His divine mission by sacrificing Himself for each of us. Perhaps she understood before anyone else that the Savior would shed His blood for each of us, because the alabaster box contained precious ointment or oil that was generally reserved for the burial of loved ones.

MATTHEW 26:6–13

6 Now when Jesus was in Bethany, in the house of Simon the leper,

7 There came unto him a woman having an alabaster box of very precious ointment, and poured it on his head, as he sat at meat.

8 But when his disciples saw it, they had indignation, saying, [Disciples] To what purpose is this waste?

9 For this ointment might have been sold for much, and given to the poor.

10 When Jesus understood it, he said unto them, [Jesus] Why trouble ye the woman? for she hath wrought a good work upon me.

11 For ye have the poor always with you; but me ye have not always.

12 For in that she hath poured this ointment on my body, she did it for my burial.

13 Verily I say unto you, Wheresoever this gospel shall be preached in the whole world, there shall also this, that this woman hath done, be told for a memorial of her.

MARK 14:3–9

3 And being in Bethany in the house of Simon the leper, as he sat at meat, there came a woman having an alabaster box of ointment of spikenard very precious; and she brake the box, and poured it on his head.

4 And there were some that had indignation within themselves, and said, [Disciples] Why was this waste of the ointment made?

5 For it might have been sold for more than three hundred pence, and have been given to the poor. And they murmured against her.

6 And Jesus said, [Jesus] Let her alone; why trouble ye her? she hath wrought a good work on me.

7 For ye have the poor with you always, and whensoever ye will ye may do them good: but me ye have not always.

8 She hath done what she could: she is come afore-
hand to anoint my body to the burying.

9 Verily I say unto you, Wheresoever this gospel shall
be preached throughout the whole world, this also that
she hath done shall be spoken of for a memorial of her.

JOHN 12:2–8

2 There they made him a supper; and Martha served:
but Lazarus was one of them that sat at the table with
him.

3 Then took Mary a pound of ointment of spikenard,
very costly, and anointed the feet of Jesus, and wiped his
feet with her hair: and the house was filled with the odour
of the ointment.

4 Then saith one of his disciples, Judas Iscariot, Simon's
son, which should betray him,

5 [Judas Iscariot] Why was not this ointment sold
for three hundred pence, and given to the poor?

6 This he said, not that he cared for the poor; but
because he was a thief, and had the bag, and bare what
was put therein.

7 Then said Jesus, [Jesus] Let her alone: against the
day of my burying hath she kept this.

8 For the poor always ye have with you; but me ye
have not always.

4

CONSPIRACY AGAINST LAZARUS

JOHN 12:9–11
Location: Bethany and Jerusalem

Summary

Many of the Jews had heard that Jesus had raised Lazarus[17] from the dead. Naturally, many of these individuals wanted to see not only Jesus, who had performed this miracle, but also Lazarus himself. Some of these individuals then believed "on Jesus" and followed Him (John 9:11). This upset the chief priests, who then conspired on how they might kill Lazarus as well.

JOHN 12: 9–11

9 Much people of the Jews therefore knew that he was there: and they came not for Jesus' sake only, but that they might see Lazarus also, whom he had raised from the dead.

10 But the chief priests consulted that they might put Lazarus also to death;

11 Because that by reason of him many of the Jews went away, and believed on Jesus.

5

PROPHECY FULFILLED

MATTHEW 21:1–5; MARK 11:1–6;
LUKE 19:28–34
Location: Mount of Olives

Summary

The Lord and His disciples were on their way to Jerusalem. When they approached Bethpage[18] and the Mount of Olives,[19] the Lord, in fulfillment of prophecy (see Zechariah 9:9), asked two of His disciples to go into the nearby village. There they would find an ass (donkey) and a colt of the ass that had never been ridden. They were to bring the colt to the Lord. The Lord told the two disciples that if the owners of the colt stopped them, they were to tell the owners that the Lord had need of him and they would comply. The disciples did as the Lord directed, and as foretold by the Lord, the owners of the ass initially stopped the disciples. When the disciples told them that the Lord had need of him, they complied.

Why did the Lord want to ride into Jerusalem on a colt of an ass rather than on a majestic horse that would typically be ridden by royalty? And why a colt that had never been ridden? In his book *Jesus the Christ*, James E. Talmage notes that the ass was "the ancient symbol of Jewish royalty" and that riding an ass was a sign of peace.[20] This suggests that the Lord was signaling to the Jewish people that He was royalty and was the Prince of Peace. As for a colt that had never been ridden, perhaps the Lord wanted to demonstrate another miracle—that not only did He have power over the physical elements of the earth, but He also had power over the animal kingdom as well.

MATTHEW 21:1–5

1 And when they drew nigh unto Jerusalem, and were come to Bethphage, unto the mount of Olives, then sent Jesus two disciples,

2 Saying unto them, [Jesus] **Go into the village over against you, and straightway ye shall find an ass tied, and a colt with her: loose them, and bring them unto me.**

3 **And if any man say ought unto you, ye shall say, The Lord hath need of them; and straightway he will send them.**

4 All this was done, that it might be fulfilled which was spoken by the prophet, saying,

5 [Zechariah (Zechariah 9:9)] **Tell ye the daughter of Sion, Behold, thy King cometh unto thee, meek, and sitting upon an ass, and a colt the foal of an ass.**

MARK 11:1–6

1 And when they came nigh to Jerusalem, unto Bethphage and Bethany, at the mount of Olives, he sendeth forth two of his disciples,

2 And saith unto them, [Jesus] **Go your way into the village over against you: and as soon as ye be entered into it, ye shall find a colt tied, whereon never man sat; loose him, and bring him.**

3 **And if any man say unto you, Why do ye this? say ye that the Lord hath need of him; and straightway he will send him hither.**

4 And they went their way, and found the colt tied by the door without in a place where two ways met; and they loose him.

5 And certain of them that stood there said unto them, [Certain Men] **What do ye, loosing the colt?**

6 And they said unto them even as Jesus had commanded: and they let them go.

LUKE 19:28–34

28 And when he had thus spoken, he went before, ascending up to Jerusalem.

29 And it came to pass, when he was come nigh to Bethphage and Bethany, at the mount called the mount of Olives, he sent two of his disciples,

30 Saying, [**Jesus**] **Go ye into the village over against you; in the which at your entering ye shall find a colt tied, whereon yet never man sat: loose him, and bring him hither.**

31 **And if any man ask you, Why do ye loose him? thus shall ye say unto him, Because the Lord hath need of him.**

32 And they that were sent went their way, and found even as he had said unto them.

33 And as they were loosing the colt, the owners thereof said unto them, [**Owners of Colt**] **Why loose ye the colt?**

34 And they said, [**Two Disciples**] **The Lord hath need of him.**

6

TRIUMPHAL ENTRY

MATTHEW 21:6–11; MARK 11:7–11;
LUKE 19:35–38; JOHN 12:12–18
Location: Jerusalem

Summary

When it came time for the Lord to go up to Jerusalem, He instructed some of His disciples to bring Him a colt that had never been ridden. The disciples obeyed, and the Lord rode the colt into the city. The people placed palm leaves and straw in front of His path and shouted, "Hosanna to the Son of David: Blessed is he that cometh in the name of the Lord; Hosanna in the highest"[21] (Matthew 21:9). These individuals revered Him as the King of Israel and the Messiah.[22] Those who loved Him and revered Him as their king had seen His mighty works and were convinced of His divine appointment. However, others, including the priests and Pharisees, hated Him and wanted to kill Him.

MATTHEW 21:6–11

6 And the disciples went, and did as Jesus commanded them,

7 And brought the ass, and the colt, and put on them their clothes, and they set him thereon.

8 And a very great multitude spread their garments in the way; others cut down branches from the trees, and strawed them in the way.

11

9 And the multitudes that went before, and that followed, cried, saying, [**Multitude**] **Hosanna to the Son of David: Blessed is he that cometh in the name of the Lord; Hosanna in the highest.**

10 And when he was come into Jerusalem, all the city was moved, saying, [**All the City**] **Who is this?**

11 And the multitude said, [**Multitude**] **This is Jesus the prophet of Nazareth of Galilee.**

MARK 11:7–11

7 And they brought the colt to Jesus, and cast their garments on him; and he sat upon him.

8 And many spread their garments in the way: and others cut down branches off the trees, and strawed them in the way.

9 And they that went before, and they that followed, cried, saying, [**Multitude**] **Hosanna; Blessed is he that cometh in the name of the Lord:**

10 Blessed be the kingdom of our father David, that cometh in the name of the Lord: Hosanna in the highest.

11 And Jesus entered into Jerusalem, and into the temple: and when he had looked round about upon all things, and now the eventide was come, he went out unto Bethany with the twelve.

LUKE 19:35–38

35 And they brought him to Jesus: and they cast their garments upon the colt, and they set Jesus thereon.

36 And as he went, they spread their clothes in the way.

37 And when he was come nigh, even now at the descent of the mount of Olives, the whole multitude of the disciples began to rejoice and praise God with a loud voice for all the mighty works that they had seen;

38 Saying, [**Multitude**] **Blessed be the King that cometh in the name of the Lord: peace in heaven, and glory in the highest.**

JOHN 12:12–18

12 On the next day much people that were come to the feast, when they heard that Jesus was coming to Jerusalem,

13 Took branches of palm trees, and went forth to meet him, and cried, [**Multitude**] **Hosanna: Blessed is the King of Israel that cometh in the name of the Lord.**

14 And Jesus, when he had found a young ass, sat thereon; as it is written,

15 Fear not, daughter of Sion: behold, thy King cometh, sitting on an ass's colt.

16 These things understood not his disciples at the first: but when Jesus was glorified, then remembered they that these things were written of him, and that they had done these things unto him.

17 The people therefore that was with him when he called Lazarus out of his grave, and raised him from the dead, bare record.

18 For this cause the people also met him, for that they heard that he had done this miracle.

7

PHARISEES DISAPPROVE

LUKE 19:39–40; JOHN 12:19
Location: Jerusalem

Summary

The Pharisees did not like that the multitude was worshipping the Lord and praising Him, and they expected the Lord to quiet the crowd and to chastise them for revering Him as the Lord. Instead of complying with their demands, the Lord pointed out that He was the Messiah and that if the people didn't acknowledge it the stones would cry out.

LUKE 19:39–40

39 And some of the Pharisees from among the multitude said unto him, [**Pharisees**] **Master, rebuke thy disciples.**

40 And he answered and said unto them, [**Jesus**] **I tell you that, if these should hold their peace, the stones would immediately cry out.**

JOHN 12:19

19 The Pharisees therefore said among themselves, [**Pharisees**] **Perceive ye how ye prevail nothing? behold, the world is gone after him.**

8

JESUS WEEPS OVER JERUSALEM

LUKE 19:41–44
Location: Near Jerusalem

Summary

As the Lord approached Jerusalem, He became sad and wept over the city. This physical emotion demonstrates His great love for the people and the community where He had spent so much time. He knew of the lost opportunity that they had squandered and the suffering that they would experience in the future because they rejected Him. He spoke of the siege of the city that would occur in the future and the destruction of the city itself. He prophesied that "they shall not leave in thee one stone upon another" (Luke 19:44). Of course, we know that in about 70 AD the Romans did lay siege to the city. Before it was all over, blood ran in the streets, and the city was decimated.

LUKE 19:41–44

41 And when he was come near, he beheld the city, and wept over it,

42 Saying, [Jesus] **If thou hadst known, even thou, at least in this thy day, the things which belong unto thy peace! but now they are hid from thine eyes.**

43 For the days shall come upon thee, that thine enemies shall cast a trench about thee, and compass thee round, and keep thee in on every side,

44 And shall lay thee even with the ground, and thy children within thee; and they shall not leave in thee one stone upon another; because thou knewest not the time of thy visitation.

9

THE FOURTH DAY BEFORE Passover

MATTHEW 21:17–18; MARK 11:12
Location: Bethany

Summary

On the morning of the fourth day before the Passover, after lodging in Bethany, Jesus returned to the city. He had not eaten and was hungry. These scriptures provide insight into the Lord's mortal body. He needed to eat and sleep just like we do.

MATTHEW 21:17–18

17 And he left them, and went out of the city into Bethany; and he lodged there.

18 Now in the morning as he returned into the city, he hungred.

MARK 11:12

12 And on the morrow, when they were come from Bethany, he was hungry.

10
FIG TREE CURSED

MATTHEW 21:18–19; MARK 11:12–14
Location: Near Bethany

Summary

After spending the night in Bethany, the Lord was hungry. He approached a fig tree[23] with healthy leaves and hoped to find figs to eat. However, He found nothing but leaves. He cursed the tree by saying, "No man eat fruit of thee hereafter for ever" (Mark 11:14). The next day (see section 13) while passing by the withered tree, the Lord taught a powerful lesson about faith. Perhaps He had that in mind when He cursed the fig tree. In any regard, it is clear that the Lord wanted to teach His disciples, and us as well, important principles about faith and the priesthood of God's power over the physical elements of the earth. This type of experience, which had occurred on many occasions with the disciples, was a powerful testimony of the Lord's omnipotence.

MATTHEW 21:18–19

18 Now in the morning as he returned into the city, he hungred.

19 And when he saw a fig tree in the way, he came to it, and found nothing thereon, but leaves only, and said unto it, [Jesus] **Let no fruit grow on thee henceforward for ever.** And presently the fig tree withered away.

MARK 11:12–14

12 And on the morrow, when they were come from Bethany, he was hungry:

13 And seeing a fig tree afar off having leaves, he came, if haply he might find any thing thereon: and when he came to it, he found nothing but leaves; for the time of figs was not yet.

14. And Jesus answered and said unto it, [**Jesus**] **No man eat fruit of thee hereafter for ever.** And his disciples heard it.

11

MONEY CHANGERS CAST OUT

MATTHEW 21:12–16; MARK 11:15–19; LUKE 19:45–48
Location: Jerusalem

Summary

After cursing the fig tree on His way to Jerusalem, the Lord went to the temple, where He cast out those who bought and sold in the temple. He overturned the moneychangers' tables and chairs and then referred to the temple as "my house." He instructed them that the temple "shall be called a house of prayer" (Matthew 21:13). After cleansing the temple, the Lord healed the blind and lame, and the children cried, "Hosanna to the Son of David" (Matthew 21:15). The scriptures also indicate that He taught daily in the temple and that the chief priests and scribes were not pleased when they observed that the people who heard the Savior teach were impressed and wanted to know more.

MATTHEW 21:12–16

12 And Jesus went into the temple of God, and cast out all them that sold and bought in the temple, and overthrew the tables of the moneychangers, and the seats of them that sold doves,

20

13 And said unto them, [Jesus] **It is written, My house shall be called the house of prayer; but ye have made it a den of thieves.**

14 And the blind and the lame came to him in the temple; and he healed them.

15 And when the chief priests and scribes saw the wonderful things that he did, and the children crying in the temple, and saying, [Children in the Temple] **Hosanna to the Son of David; they were sore displeased,**

16 And said unto him, [Chief Priests] **Hearest thou what these say?** And Jesus saith unto them, [Jesus] **Yea; have ye never read, Out of the mouth of babes and sucklings thou hast perfected praise?**

MARK 11:15–19

15 And they come to Jerusalem: and Jesus went into the temple, and began to cast out them that sold and bought in the temple, and overthrew the tables of the money-changers, and the seats of them that sold doves;

16 And would not suffer that any man should carry any vessel through the temple.

17 And he taught, saying unto them, [Jesus] **Is it not written, My house shall be called of all nations the house of prayer? but ye have made it a den of thieves.**

18 And the scribes and chief priests heard it, and sought how they might destroy him: for they feared him, because all the people was astonished at his doctrine.

19 And when even was come, he went out of the city.

LUKE 19:45–48

45 And he went into the temple, and began to cast out them that sold therein, and them that bought;

46 Saying unto them, [Jesus] **It is written, My house is the house of prayer: but ye have made it a den of thieves.**

47 And he taught daily in the temple. But the chief priests and the scribes and the chief of the people sought to destroy him,

48 And could not find what they might do: for all the people were very attentive to hear him.

12

THE THIRD DAY BEFORE PASSOVER

MARK 11:19–20
Location: Near Jerusalem

Summary

On the fourth day before Passover, the Lord left the city, probably to find a place to eat and sleep. On the next morning, which would have been the third day before Passover, the Lord headed back to Jerusalem. On the way, He passed by the fig tree that He had cursed the previous day.

MARK 11:19–20

19 And when even was come, he went out of the city.

20 And in the morning, as they passed by, they saw the fig tree dried up from the roots.

13

WITHERED FIG TREE AND DISCOURSE ON FAITH

MATTHEW 21:20–22; MARK 11:20–26
Location: Near Jerusalem

Summary

The disciples saw that the fig tree had withered, and Peter pointed this out to the Lord. The Lord then taught the disciples about faith, pointing out that if they had faith, they could do great things as well. For instance, they could cause a tree to wither or a mountain to move. The Lord also tied faith to prayer and taught that "when ye pray, believe that ye receive them, and ye shall have them" (Mark 11:24). In other words, when we have righteous desires and pray for them, we should expect an answer, if we ask in faith.

MATTHEW 21:20–22

20 And when the disciples saw it, they marveled, saying, [Disciples] **How soon is the fig tree away!**

21 Jesus answered and said unto them, [**Jesus**] **Verily I say unto you, If ye have faith, and doubt not, ye shall not only do this which is done to the fig tree, but also if ye shall say unto this mountain, Be thou removed, and be thou cast into the sea; it shall be done.**

22 **And all things, whatsoever ye shall ask in prayer, believing ye shall receive.**

MARK 11:20–26

20 And in the morning, as they passed by, they saw the fig tree dried up from the roots.

21 And Peter calling to remembrance saith unto him, [Peter] Master, behold, the fig tree which thou cursedst is withered away.

22 And Jesus answering saith unto them, [Jesus] Have faith in God.

23 For verily I say unto you, That whosoever shall say unto this mountain, Be thou removed, and be thou cast into the sea; and shall not doubt in his heart, but shall believe that those things which he saith shall come to pass; he shall have whatsoever he saith.

24 Therefore I say unto you, What things soever ye desire, when ye pray, believe that ye receive them, and ye shall have them.

25 And when ye stand praying, forgive, if ye have ought against any: that your Father also which is in heaven may forgive you your trespasses.

26 But if ye do not forgive, neither will your Father which is in heaven forgive your trespasses.

14

PRIESTS CHALLENGE JESUS' AUTHORITY

MATTHEW 21:23–27; MARK 11:27–33; LUKE 20:1–8
Location: Temple

Summary

The Savior was teaching in the temple, and the chief priests, scribes, and elders came to Him to challenge His authority. They asked Him outright where He got His authority. He countered by asking them if John the Baptist's baptism was authorized by heaven. They realized that this put them in a precarious situation, for they were in trouble whether they answered yes or no. For example, if they answered yes, then they would have to admit that Jesus was the Christ, which is what John had taught. If they answered no, then they would incur the wrath of the people, for the people loved John and considered him a prophet. Why were the chief priests and scribes so headstrong and unwilling to realize the authenticity of the Savior? Are we the same way?

MATTHEW 21:23–27

23 And when he was come into the temple, the chief priests and the elders of the people came unto him as he was teaching, and said, **[Chief Priests and Elders] By what authority doest thou these things? and who gave thee this authority?**

24 And Jesus answered and said unto them, [Jesus] I also will ask you one thing, which if ye tell me, I in like wise will tell you by what authority I do these things.

25 The baptism of John, whence was it? from heaven, or of men? And they reasoned with themselves, saying, [Chief Priests and Elders] If we shall say, From heaven; he will say unto us, Why did ye not then believe him?

26 But if we shall say, Of men; we fear the people; for all hold John as a prophet.

27 And they answered Jesus, and said, [Chief Priests and Elders] We cannot tell. And he said unto them, [Jesus] Neither tell I you by what authority I do these things.

MARK 11:27–33

27 And they come again to Jerusalem: and as he was walking in the temple, there come to him the chief priests, and the scribes, and the elders,

28 And say unto him, [Chief Priests and Elders] By what authority doest thou these things? and who gave thee this authority to do these things?

29 And Jesus answered and said unto them, [Jesus] I will also ask of you one question, and answer me, and I will tell you by what authority I do these things.

30 The baptism of John, was it from heaven, or of men? answer me.

31 And they reasoned with themselves, saying, [Chief Priests and Elders] If we shall say, From heaven; he will say, Why then did ye not believe him?

32 But if we shall say, Of men; they feared the people: for all men counted John, that he was a prophet indeed.

33 And they answered and said unto Jesus, [Chief Priests and Elders] We cannot tell. And Jesus answering saith unto them, [Jesus] Neither do I tell you by what authority I do these things.

LUKE 20:1–8

1 And it came to pass, that on one of those days, as he taught the people in the temple, and preached the gospel,

the chief priests and the scribes came upon him with the elders,

2 And spake unto him, saying, [**Chief Priests and Elders**] **Tell us, by what authority doest thou these things? or who is he that gave thee this authority?**

3 And he answered and said unto them, [**Jesus**] **I will also ask you one thing; and answer me:**

4 **The baptism of John, was it from heaven, or of men?**

5 And they reasoned with themselves, saying, [**Chief Priests and Elders**] **If we shall say, From heaven; he will say, Why then believed ye him not?**

6 But and if we say, Of men; all the people will stone us: for they be persuaded that John was a prophet.

7 And they answered, that they could not tell whence it was.

8 And Jesus said unto them, [**Jesus**] **Neither tell I you by what authority I do these things.**

15

PARABLE: TWO SONS

MATTHEW 21:28–32
Location: Temple

Summary

While in the temple in Jerusalem, the Lord taught the chief priests, scribes, and elders an important lesson about repentance by telling the parable of two sons. A man who had two sons asked them individually to go work in the vineyard. The first son refused initially but then repented and did as his father wanted. The second son said that he would go to work but then didn't. The Savior asked the group He was teaching who did the will of the father—the first or second son? They answered that they believed the first son did the will of the father. Then the Savior taught them that they were like the second son because after John the Baptist taught them, they did not repent and follow the will of the Father. However, the publicans and harlots, after hearing the words of John, repented and did the will of the Father. This parable teaches that it is never too late to repent and do the will of the Father.

MATTHEW 21: 28–32

[Jesus] 28 But what think ye? A certain man had two sons; and he came to the first, and said, Son, go work to day in my vineyard.

29 He answered and said, I will not: but afterward he repented, and went.

30 And he came to the second, and said likewise. And he answered and said, I go, sir: and went not.

31 Whether of them twain did the will of his father? They say unto him, [Chief Priests, Scribes, and Elders] The first. Jesus saith unto them, [Jesus] Verily I say unto you, That the publicans and the harlots go into the kingdom of God before you.

32 For John came unto you in the way of righteousness, and ye believed him not: but the publicans and the harlots believed him: and ye, when ye had seen it, repented not afterward, that ye might believe him.

16

PARABLE: THE WICKED HUSBANDMAN

MATTHEW 21:33–46; MARK 12:1–12; LUKE 20:9–19
Location: Temple

Summary

The parable of the wicked husbandman teaches important principles about the relationship between the Father (Heavenly Father), the Son (Jesus), and the Jewish people. The essence of the parable is that the Father (a certain man) had built a vineyard (the earth) and turned it over to the husbandman (the Jewish people) to care for it. After a while, the Father (a certain man) sent servants (prophets) to assist in the vineyard and gather the fruit that had grown. Rather than respect the owner of the vineyard and receive the servant, the husbandman killed the servant (the prophet) and others who were also sent so he could keep the fruit to himself. The Father (a certain man) then thought if he sent his son (Jesus) that the husbandman (the Jewish people) would respect him and not treat him how they had treated the servants. But that did not happen. They killed the son as well. Then the Savior asked, "What shall the Lord of the vineyard do to the husbandman?"

They answered, "He shall destroy the husbandman (the Jewish people) and give the vineyard to another."

Then the Savior said, "What is this then that is written, The stone which builders rejected, the same is become the head of the corner?

Whosoever shall fall upon that stone shall be broken; but on whomsoever it shall fall, it will grind him to powder" (Matthew 21:42).

The stone represents the Savior and what happens to those who oppose Him. They are ground to powder and do not prosper. This parable provides a clear directive that opposing the Savior and His teachings leads to bad outcomes. We have to embrace the Savior and His teachings and ordinances to enjoy all the blessings of the gospel. Being contrary and rebellious does us no good. We will either be broken or ground to powder.

MATTHEW 21:33–46

33 [Jesus] Hear another parable: There was a certain householder, which planted a vineyard, and hedged it round about, and digged a winepress in it, and built a tower, and let it out to husbandmen, and went into a far country:

34 And when the time of the fruit drew near, he sent his servants to the husbandmen, that they might receive the fruits of it.

35 And the husbandmen took his servants, and beat one, and killed another, and stoned another.

36 Again, he sent other servants more than the first: and they did unto them likewise.

37 But last of all he sent unto them his son, saying, They will reverence my son.

38 But when the husbandmen saw the son, they said among themselves, This is the heir; come, let us kill him, and let us seize on his inheritance.

39 And they caught him, and cast him out of the vineyard, and slew him.

40 When the lord therefore of the vineyard cometh, what will he do unto those husbandmen?

41 They say unto him, He will miserably destroy those wicked men, and will let out his vineyard unto other husbandmen, which shall render him the fruits in their seasons.

42 Jesus saith unto them, [Jesus] Did ye never read in the scriptures, The stone which the builders rejected, the same is become the head of the corner: this is the Lord's doing, and it is marvellous in our eyes?

43 Therefore say I unto you, The kingdom of God shall be taken from you, and given to a nation bringing forth the fruits thereof.

44 And whosoever shall fall on this stone shall be broken: but on whomsoever it shall fall, it will grind him to powder.

45 And when the chief priests and Pharisees had heard his parables, they perceived that he spake of them.

46 But when they sought to lay hands on him, they feared the multitude, because they took him for a prophet.

JST, MATTHEW 21:47–56
Compare Matthew 21:45–46.

Jesus declares that He is the chief cornerstone. The gospel is offered to the Jews and then to the Gentiles. The wicked will be destroyed when Jesus returns.

47 And when the chief priests and Pharisees had heard his parables, they perceived that he spake of them.

48 And they said among themselves, Shall this man think that he alone can spoil this great kingdom? And they were angry with him.

49 But when they sought to lay hands on him, they feared the multitude, because they learned that the multitude took him for a prophet.

50 And now his disciples came to him, and Jesus said unto them, [Jesus] Marvel ye at the words of the parable which I spake unto them?

51 Verily, I say unto you, I am the stone, and those wicked ones reject me.

52 I am the head of the corner. These Jews shall fall upon me, and shall be broken.

53 And the kingdom of God shall be taken from them, and shall be given to a nation bringing forth the fruits thereof; (meaning the Gentiles.)

54 Wherefore, on whomsoever this stone shall fall, it shall grind him to powder.

55 And when the Lord therefore of the vineyard cometh, he will destroy those miserable, wicked men,

and will let again his vineyard unto other husbandmen, even in the last days, who shall render him the fruits in their seasons.

56 And then understood they the parable which he spake unto them, that the Gentiles should be destroyed also, when the Lord should descend out of heaven to reign in his vineyard, which is the earth and the inhabitants thereof.

MARK 12:1–12

1 And he began to speak unto them by parables. [**Jesus**] A certain man planted a vineyard, and set an hedge about it, and digged a place for the winefat, and built a tower, and let it out to husbandmen, and went into a far country.

2 And at the season he sent to the husbandmen a servant, that he might receive from the husbandmen of the fruit of the vineyard.

3 And they caught him, and beat him, and sent him away empty.

4 And again he sent unto them another servant; and at him they cast stones, and wounded him in the head, and sent him away shamefully handled.

5 And again he sent another; and him they killed, and many others; beating some, and killing some.

6 Having yet therefore one son, his wellbeloved, he sent him also last unto them, saying, They will reverence my son.

7 But those husbandmen said among themselves, This is the heir; come, let us kill him, and the inheritance shall be ours.

8 And they took him, and killed him, and cast him out of the vineyard.

9 What shall therefore the lord of the vineyard do? he will come and destroy the husbandmen, and will give the vineyard unto others.

10 And have ye not read this scripture [Psalm 118:22–23]; The stone which the builders rejected is become the head of the corner:

11 This was the Lord's doing, and it is marvellous in our eyes?

12 And they sought to lay hold on him, but feared the people: for they knew that he had spoken the parable against them: and they left him, and went their way.

LUKE 20:9–19

9 Then began he to speak to the people this parable; [Jesus] A certain man planted a vineyard, and let it forth to husbandmen, and went into a far country for a long time.

10 And at the season he sent a servant to the husbandmen, that they should give him of the fruit of the vineyard: but the husbandmen beat him, and sent him away empty.

11 And again he sent another servant: and they beat him also, and entreated him shamefully, and sent him away empty.

12 And again he sent a third: and they wounded him also, and cast him out.

13 Then said the lord of the vineyard, What shall I do? I will send my beloved son: it may be they will reverence him when they see him.

14 But when the husbandmen saw him, they reasoned among themselves, saying, This is the heir: come, let us kill him, that the inheritance may be ours.

15 So they cast him out of the vineyard, and killed him. What therefore shall the lord of the vineyard do unto them?

16 He shall come and destroy these husbandmen, and shall give the vineyard to others. [Chief Priest, Scribes, and Elders] And when they heard it, they said, God forbid.

17 And he beheld them, and said, [Jesus] What is this then that is written, The stone which the builders rejected, the same is become the head of the corner?

18 Whosoever shall fall upon that stone shall be broken; but on whomsoever it shall fall, it will grind him to powder.

19 And the chief priests and the scribes the same hour sought to lay hands on him; and they feared the people: for they perceived that he had spoken this parable against them.

17

PARABLE: WEDDING OF A KING'S SON

MATTHEW 22:1–14
Location: Temple

Summary

Jesus taught the parable of the wedding of the king's son in the temple. The story begins with the king sending forth his servants to notify the guests that all was ready, but the guests would not come. The king sent his servants again to notify the guests that all was truly ready and to come to the wedding. This time he told the servants to tell the people about the lengths that he had gone to in preparing the dinner for the wedding. Still the people made light of it and went about with their busy life of farming and business. Some of the invitees even persecuted and killed the king's servants. The king became angry and sent his armies to destroy them and to burn their cities. Then he sent his servants to extend an invitation to everyone else so that the wedding would have guests.

The servants did as the king requested and gathered all that they found, "both bad and good, and the wedding was furnished with guests" (Matthew 22:10). When the king came into the wedding, he noticed that one of the men was not wearing a wedding garment. "And he saith unto him, Friend, how camest thou in hither not having a wedding garment? And he was speechless. Then said the king to the servants, Bind him hand

and foot, and take him away, and cast him into outer darkness; there shall be weeping and gnashing of teeth. For many are called, but few are chosen" (Matthew 22:12–14).

We can learn much from this powerful parable. Perhaps one lesson we learn is that the Lord invites people from all backgrounds, but He expects them to change and be fit for his kingdom.

Doctrine and Covenants 121:34–46 provides more insight into the last line of this parable by providing the following: "Behold, there are many called, but few are chosen. And why are they not chosen? Because their hearts are set so much upon the things of this world, and aspire to the honors of men, that they do not learn this one lesson—That the rights of the priesthood are inseparably connected with the powers of heaven, and that the powers of heaven cannot be controlled nor handled only upon the principles of righteousness."

MATTHEW 22:1–14

1 And Jesus answered and spake unto them again by parables, and said,

2 [Jesus] The kingdom of heaven is like unto a certain king, which made a marriage for his son,

3 And sent forth his servants to call them that were bidden to the wedding: and they would not come.

4 Again, he sent forth other servants, saying, Tell them which are bidden, Behold, I have prepared my dinner: my oxen and my fatlings are killed, and all things are ready: come unto the marriage.

5 But they made light of it, and went their ways, one to his farm, another to his merchandise:

6 And the remnant took his servants, and entreated them spitefully, and slew them.

7 But when the king heard thereof, he was wroth: and he sent forth his armies, and destroyed those murderers, and burned up their city.

8 Then saith he to his servants, The wedding is ready, but they which were bidden were not worthy.

9 Go ye therefore into the highways, and as many as ye shall find, bid to the marriage.

10 So those servants went out into the highways, and

gathered together all as many as they found, both bad and good: and the wedding was furnished with guests.

11 And when the king came in to see the guests, he saw there a man which had not on a wedding garment:

12 And he saith unto him, Friend, how camest thou in hither not having a wedding garment? And he was speechless.

13 Then said the king to the servants, Bind him hand and foot, and take him away, and cast him into outer darkness; there shall be weeping and gnashing of teeth.

14 For many are called, but few are chosen.

18

QUESTION ABOUT TRIBUTE

MATTHEW 22:15–22; MARK 12:13–17;
LUKE 20:20–26
Location: Temple

Summary

At this time, the Jewish people were under Roman rule and subjected to Roman laws. The Pharisees hated Jesus, and they thought that if they could find Him in violation of the laws of the government that He would then be subject to Roman punishment. In this setting they wanted the Lord to say that the only true leader is God and that subjection to any other person or entity is wrong. However, the Lord was able to discern their thoughts and was able to counter with the seminal statement, "Render unto Caesar that which is Caesars and that which is God's to God" (Matthew 22:21).

The Lord's response teaches us that we can be subject to laws of the land. Even though they may be contrary to the laws of God, we should follow them as long as we also have faith and follow the teachings of God when we can. It doesn't have to be an either/or situation. We can live in the world but not be of the world.

MATTHEW 22:15–22

15 Then went the Pharisees, and took counsel how they might entangle him in his talk.

16 And they sent out unto him their disciples with the Herodians, saying, [Pharisees] **Master, we know that thou art true, and teachest the way of God in truth, neither carest thou for any man: for thou regardest not the person of men.**

17 **Tell us therefore, What thinkest thou? Is it lawful to give tribute unto Cæsar, or not?**

18 But Jesus perceived their wickedness, and said, [Jesus] **Why tempt ye me, ye hypocrites?**

19 **Shew me the tribute money.** And they brought unto him a penny.

20 And he saith unto them, [Jesus] **Whose is this image and superscription?**

21 They say unto him, [Pharisees] **Cæsar's.** Then saith he unto them, [Jesus] **Render therefore unto Cæsar the things which are Cæsar's; and unto God the things that are God's.**

22 When they had heard these words, they marvelled, and left him, and went their way.

MARK 12:13–17

13 And they send unto him certain of the Pharisees and of the Herodians, to catch him in his words.

14 And when they were come, they say unto him, [Pharisees] **Master, we know that thou art true, and carest for no man: for thou regardest not the person of men, but teachest the way of God in truth: Is it lawful to give tribute to Cæsar, or not?**

15 **Shall we give, or shall we not give?** But he, knowing their hypocrisy, said unto them, [Jesus] **Why tempt ye me? bring me a penny, that I may see it.**

16 And they brought it. And he saith unto them, [Jesus] **Whose is this image and superscription?** And they said unto him, [Pharisees] **Cæsar's.**

17 And Jesus answering said unto them, [Jesus] **Render to Cæsar the things that are Cæsar's, and to God the things that are God's.** And they marvelled at him.

LUKE 20:20–26

20 And they watched him, and sent forth spies, which should feign themselves just men, that they might take hold of his words, that so they might deliver him unto the power and authority of the governor.

21 And they asked him, saying, [Jesus] **Master, we know that thou sayest and teachest rightly, neither acceptest thou the person of any, but teachest the way of God truly:**

22 Is it lawful for us to give tribute unto Cæsar, or no?

23 But he perceived their craftiness, and said unto them, [Jesus] **Why tempt ye me?**

24 Shew me a penny. Whose image and super-scription hath it? They answered and said, [Pharisees] **Cæsar's.**

25 And he said unto them, [Jesus] **Render therefore unto Cæsar the things which be Cæsar's, and unto God the things which be God's.**

26 And they could not take hold of his words before the people: and they marvelled at his answer, and held their peace.

19

MARRIAGE AND THE RESURRECTION: SADDUCEES

MATTHEW 22:23–33; MARK 12:18–27;
LUKE 20:27–38

Location: Temple

Summary

The Sadducees[24] came to the Lord with a question about marriage[25] and the resurrection.[26] They did not believe in the resurrection, so this was probably meant to entrap the Lord in His teachings. Also, as noted in the Bible Dictionary (under "Sadducees"), "they refused also to accept the doctrine of immortality as a necessary part of the Jewish faith." They posed a scenario wherein a man dies without children and his brother takes his wife to raise up seed to his brother but then dies childless. This same situation occurs through seven brothers.

Given that, whose wife is she in the next life? The scriptures provide the following: "And Jesus answering said unto them, The children of this world marry, and are given in marriage: But they which shall be accounted worthy to obtain that world, and the resurrection from the dead, neither marry, nor are given in marriage: Neither can they die anymore: for they are equal unto the angels; and are the children of God, being the children

41

of the resurrection. Now that the dead are raised, even Moses shewed at the bush, when he called the Lord the God of Abraham, and the God of Isaac, and the God of Jacob. For he is not a God of the dead, but of the living: for all live unto him" (Luke 20:34–38).

The above teachings by themselves are confusing. However, if we read them in the context of the restored gospel and the scriptures provided in this dispensation, then we get a better idea of what the Lord was teaching. Doctrine and Covenants sections 131 and 132 provide insight into the new and everlasting covenant of marriage. The Lord makes clear in these sections that if we marry in this life under the laws of the land, the marriage does not continue after death. But, if we enter into the new and everlasting covenant of marriage by one who holds the authority to seal us, and if the sealing is ratified by the Holy Spirit of promise, then the marriage is an eternal union that lasts eternally. These same blessings are offered to all of God's children in this life or the next, but only to the righteous.

Elder Bruce R. McConkie said the following:

> There is neither marrying nor giving in marriage in heaven for those to whom Jesus was speaking; for those who do not even believe in a resurrection, let alone all the other saving truths; the manner of the world; for the great masses of unrepentant mankind. All of these will fall short of gaining the fullness of reward hereafter. What then is their state? They will not be "gods" and thus have exaltation; their inheritance will be in a lessor degree of glory. As Jesus said to the Sadducees, "they are as the angels of God in heaven," "for they are equal unto the angels." As he said, in more detail and with greater plainness to Joseph Smith, they "are appointed angels in heaven; which angels are ministering servants, to minister for those who are worthy of a far more, and an exceeding, and an eternal weight of glory. For these angels did not abide my law; therefore, they cannot be enlarged, but remain separately and singly, without exaltation, in their saved condition, to all eternity; and from henceforth are not gods but are angels of God forever and ever." (D. & C. 132:5–17). Thus, in the resurrection, the unmarried remain everlastingly as angels or servants, but the married gain exaltation and godhood.
>
> This latter group consists of those who enter into that "order of the priesthood: named "the new and everlasting covenant of marriage," and who then keep the terms and conditions of that eternal covenant. (D. & C. 131:1–4) It consists also of those who lived on earth under circumstances which prevented them from making the covenant for themselves personally, but who would have done so had the opportunity been afforded. For all such, on the just and equitable principles of salvation and exaltation for the dead, the ordinances will be performed vicariously in the temples of God,

so that no blessing will ever be denied to any worthy person. And for that matter, there is no revelation, either ancient or modern, which says there is neither marrying nor giving in marriage in heaven itself for righteous people. All that the revelations set forth is that such is denied to the Sadducees and other worldly and ungodly people."[27]

MATTHEW 22:23–33

23 The same day came to him the Sadducees, which say that there is no resurrection, and asked him,

24 Saying, [Sadducees] Master, Moses said, If a man die, having no children, his brother shall marry his wife, and raise up seed unto his brother.

25 Now there were with us seven brethren: and the first, when he had married a wife, deceased, and, having no issue, left his wife unto his brother:

26 Likewise the second also, and the third, unto the seventh.

27 And last of all the woman died also.

28 Therefore in the resurrection whose wife shall she be of the seven? for they all had her.

29 Jesus answered and said unto them, [Jesus] Ye do err, not knowing the scriptures, nor the power of God.

30 For in the resurrection they neither marry, nor are given in marriage, but are as the angels of God in heaven.

31 But as touching the resurrection of the dead, have ye not read that which was spoken unto you by God, saying,

32 I am the God of Abraham, and the God of Isaac, and the God of Jacob? God is not the God of the dead, but of the living.

33 And when the multitude heard this, they were astonished at his doctrine.

MARK 12:18–27

18 Then come unto him the Sadducees, which say there is no resurrection; and they asked him, saying,

19 [Sadducees] Master, Moses wrote unto us, If a man's brother die, and leave his wife behind him, and

leave no children, that his brother should take his wife, and raise up seed unto his brother.

20 Now there were seven brethren: and the first took a wife, and dying left no seed.

21 And the second took her, and died, neither left he any seed: and the third likewise.

22 And the seven had her, and left no seed: last of all the woman died also.

23 In the resurrection therefore, when they shall rise, whose wife shall she be of them? for the seven had her to wife.

24 And Jesus answering said unto them, [Jesus] Do ye not therefore err, because ye know not the scriptures, neither the power of God?

25 For when they shall rise from the dead, they neither marry, nor are given in marriage; but are as the angels which are in heaven.

26 And as touching the dead, that they rise: have ye not read in the book of Moses, how in the bush God spake unto him, saying, I am the God of Abraham, and the God of Isaac, and the God of Jacob?

27 He is not the God of the dead, but the God of the living: ye therefore do greatly err.

LUKE 20:27–38

27 Then came to him certain of the Sadducees, which deny that there is any resurrection; and they asked him,

28 Saying, [Sadducees] Master, Moses wrote unto us, If any man's brother die, having a wife, and he die without children, that his brother should take his wife, and raise up seed unto his brother.

29 There were therefore seven brethren: and the first took a wife, and died without children.

30 And the second took her to wife, and he died childless.

31 And the third took her; and in like manner the seven also: and they left no children, and died.

32 Last of all the woman died also.

33 Therefore in the resurrection whose wife of them is she? for seven had her to wife.

34 And Jesus answering said unto them, [**Jesus**] The children of this world marry, and are given in marriage:

35 But they which shall be accounted worthy to obtain that world, and the resurrection from the dead, neither marry, nor are given in marriage:

36 Neither can they die any more: for they are equal unto the angels; and are the children of God, being the children of the resurrection.

37 Now that the dead are raised, even Moses shewed at the bush, when he calleth the Lord the God of Abraham, and the God of Isaac, and the God of Jacob.

38 For he is not a God of the dead, but of the living: for all live unto him.

20

GREAT COMMANDMENT: PHARISEES

MATTHEW 22:34–40; MARK 12:28–34
Location: Temple

Summary

The Lord was teaching in the temple when one of the scribes[28] (lawyers)[29] asked Him which law was the most important. Matthew said that this question was in the spirit of tempting the Lord. The Lord responded and taught the order of importance. The commandment that is most important is our love for God, and the second is not far from it—to love our neighbors as ourselves.

The first great commandment encompasses all the commandments. If we truly love the Lord, we will love His word and His commandments (which are given in love and for our benefit), and we will seek to keep all of them. The second commandment of loving others as we love ourselves encompasses everything else that we need to know and do. If we truly love others, we will seek that which is best for them and serve them and bless them. The Lord's response to the scribe was beautiful and all-encompassing. There couldn't have been a better response.

MATTHEW 22:34–40

34 But when the Pharisees had heard that he had put the Sadducees to silence, they were gathered together.

46

35 Then one of them, which was a lawyer, asked him a question, tempting him, and saying,

36 [Pharisees] Master, which is the great commandment in the law?

37 Jesus said unto him, [Jesus] Thou shalt love the Lord thy God with all thy heart, and with all thy soul, and with all thy mind.

38 This is the first and great commandment.

39 And the second is like unto it, Thou shalt love thy neighbour as thyself.

40 On these two commandments hang all the law and the prophets.

MARK 12:28–34

28 And one of the scribes came, and having heard them reasoning together, and perceiving that he had answered them well, asked him, [Scribes] Which is the first commandment of all?

29 And Jesus answered him, [Jesus] The first of all the commandments is, Hear, O Israel; The Lord our God is one Lord:

30 And thou shalt love the Lord thy God with all thy heart, and with all thy soul, and with all thy mind, and with all thy strength: this is the first commandment.

31 And the second is like, namely this, Thou shalt love thy neighbour as thyself. There is none other commandment greater than these.

32 And the scribe said unto him, [Scribe] Well, Master, thou hast said the truth: for there is one God; and there is none other but he:

33 And to love him with all the heart, and with all the understanding, and with all the soul, and with all the strength, and to love his neighbour as himself, is more than all whole burnt offerings and sacrifices.

34 And when Jesus saw that he answered discreetly, he said unto him, [Jesus] Thou art not far from the kingdom of God. And no man after that durst ask him any question.

21

HOW IS CHRIST BOTH DAVID'S LORD AND SON?

MATTHEW 22:41–46; MARK 12:35–37;
LUKE 20:39–44
Location: Temple

Summary

While in the temple, Jesus asked the Pharisees how Christ could be both David's Son and David's Lord. This question must have been quite confusing to those who didn't understand or believe in the premortal life. Jehovah was Lord in the premortal life, and Jesus Christ (Jehovah) was born and received a mortal body through the lineage of David. The Savior wanted it clear that He was both David's son and His Lord.

MATTHEW 22:41–46

41 While the Pharisees were gathered together, Jesus asked them,

42 Saying, [**Jesus**] **What think ye of Christ? whose son is he?** They say unto him, [**Pharisees**] **The Son of David.**

43 He saith unto them, [**Jesus**] **How then doth David in spirit call him Lord, saying,**

44 **The Lord said unto my Lord, Sit thou on my right hand, till I make thine enemies thy footstool?**

45 If David then call him Lord, how is he his son?

46 And no man was able to answer him a word, neither durst any man from that day forth ask him any more questions.

MARK 12:35–37

35 And Jesus answered and said, while he taught in the temple, [Jesus] How say the scribes that Christ is the Son of David?

36 For David himself said by the Holy Ghost, The Lord said to my Lord, Sit thou on my right hand, till I make thine enemies thy footstool.

37 David therefore himself calleth him Lord; and whence is he then his son? And the common people heard him gladly.

LUKE 20:39–44

39 Then certain of the scribes answering said, [Scribes] Master, thou hast well said.

40 And after that they durst not ask him any question at all.

41 And he said unto them, [Jesus] How say they that Christ is David's son?

42 And David himself saith in the book of Psalms, The Lord said unto my Lord, Sit thou on my right hand,

43 Till I make thine enemies thy footstool.

44 David therefore calleth him Lord, how is he then his son?

22

DENUNCIATION OF HYPOCRISY

MATTHEW 23:1–36; MARK 12:38–40;
LUKE 20:45–47
Location: Temple

Summary

While teaching in the temple, the Savior taught His disciples about hypocrisy and the just reward for those who practice it. The verses in this section provide a sharp rebuke to all who practice hypocrisy.[30] For instance, Matthew 23:24 says, "Ye blind guides, which strain at a gnat, and swallow a camel." Also, in verse 27 the Lord teaches, "Woe unto you, scribes and Pharisees, hypocrites! for ye are like unto whited sepulchres, which indeed appear beautiful outward, but are within full of dead men's bones, and of all uncleanness."

MATTHEW 23:1–36

1 Then spake Jesus to the multitude, and to his disciples,

2 Saying, [Jesus] The scribes and the Pharisees sit in Moses' seat:

3 All therefore whatsoever they bid you observe, that observe and do; but do not ye after their works: for they say, and do not.

50

4 For they bind heavy burdens and grievous to be borne, and lay them on men's shoulders; but they themselves will not move them with one of their fingers.

5 But all their works they do for to be seen of men: they make broad their phylacteries, and enlarge the borders of their garments,

6 And love the uppermost rooms at feasts, and the chief seats in the synagogues,

7 And greetings in the markets, and to be called of men, Rabbi, Rabbi.

8 But be not ye called Rabbi: for one is your Master, even Christ; and all ye are brethren.

9 And call no man your father upon the earth: for one is your Father, which is in heaven.

10 Neither be ye called masters: for one is your Master, even Christ.

11 But he that is greatest among you shall be your servant.

12 And whosoever shall exalt himself shall be abased; and he that shall humble himself shall be exalted.

13 But woe unto you, scribes and Pharisees, hypocrites! for ye shut up the kingdom of heaven against men: for ye neither go in yourselves, neither suffer ye them that are entering to go in.

14 Woe unto you, scribes and Pharisees, hypocrites! for ye devour widows' houses, and for a pretence make long prayer: therefore ye shall receive the greater damnation.

15 Woe unto you, scribes and Pharisees, hypocrites! for ye compass sea and land to make one proselyte, and when he is made, ye make him twofold more the child of hell than yourselves.

16 Woe unto you, ye blind guides, which say, Whosoever shall swear by the temple, it is nothing; but whosoever shall swear by the gold of the temple, he is a debtor!

17 Ye fools and blind: for whether is greater, the gold, or the temple that sanctifieth the gold?

18 And, Whosoever shall swear by the altar, it is nothing; but whosoever sweareth by the gift that is upon it, he is guilty.

19 Ye fools and blind: for whether is greater, the gift, or the altar that sanctifieth the gift?

20 Whoso therefore shall swear by the altar, sweareth by it, and by all things thereon.

21 And whoso shall swear by the temple, sweareth by it, and by him that dwelleth therein.

22 And he that shall swear by heaven, sweareth by the throne of God, and by him that sitteth thereon.

23 Woe unto you, scribes and Pharisees, hypocrites! for ye pay tithe of mint and anise and cummin, and have omitted the weightier matters of the law, judgment, mercy, and faith: these ought ye to have done, and not to leave the other undone.

24 Ye blind guides, which strain at a gnat, and swallow a camel.

25 Woe unto you, scribes and Pharisees, hypocrites! for ye make clean the outside of the cup and of the platter, but within they are full of extortion and excess.

26 Thou blind Pharisee, cleanse first that which is within the cup and platter, that the outside of them may be clean also.

27 Woe unto you, scribes and Pharisees, hypocrites! for ye are like unto whited sepulchres, which indeed appear beautiful outward, but are within full of dead men's bones, and of all uncleanness.

28 Even so ye also outwardly appear righteous unto men, but within ye are full of hypocrisy and iniquity.

29 Woe unto you, scribes and Pharisees, hypocrites! because ye build the tombs of the prophets, and garnish the sepulchres of the righteous,

30 And say, If we had been in the days of our fathers, we would not have been partakers with them in the blood of the prophets.

31 Wherefore ye be witnesses unto yourselves, that ye are the children of them which killed the prophets.

32 Fill ye up then the measure of your fathers.

33 Ye serpents, ye generation of vipers, how can ye escape the damnation of hell?

34 Wherefore, behold, I send unto you prophets, and wise men, and scribes: and some of them ye shall kill and crucify; and some of them shall ye scourge in your synagogues, and persecute them from city to city:

35 That upon you may come all the righteous blood shed upon the earth, from the blood of righteous Abel unto the blood of Zacharias son of Barachias, whom ye slew between the temple and the altar.

36 Verily I say unto you, All these things shall come upon this generation.

MARK 12:38–40

38 And he said unto them in his doctrine, [Jesus] Beware of the scribes, which love to go in long clothing, and love salutations in the marketplaces,

39 And the chief seats in the synagogues, and the uppermost rooms at feasts:

40 Which devour widows' houses, and for a pretence make long prayers: these shall receive greater damnation.

LUKE 20:45–47

45 Then in the audience of all the people he said unto his disciples,

46 [Jesus] Beware of the scribes, which desire to walk in long robes, and love greetings in the markets, and the highest seats in the synagogues, and the chief rooms at feasts;

47 Which devour widows' houses, and for a shew make long prayers: the same shall receive greater damnation.

23
WIDOW'S MITE

MARK 12:41–44; LUKE 21:1–4
Location: Temple

Summary

While standing next to the treasury in the temple, the Savior observed people coming in and contributing money. Many of the rich contributed much, but a poor widow contributed only two mites.[31] When the Savior observed this, He gathered His disciples near Him and taught them an important lesson: "This poor widow hath cast more in, than all they which have cast into the treasury" (Mark 12:43). Why would He say that? How could such a small contribution be greater than a much larger one? Jesus said, "For all they did cast in of their abundance; but she of her want did cast in all that she had, even all her living" (Mark 12:44).

It is clear, of course, that the widow did not contribute more money than the rich. But in a relative sense, she did. I think that the Savior paused and pointed this out to His disciples so He could teach them an important lesson, namely, that we are all in different circumstances and that it is not what we have or what we give, so to speak, but the relative amount of our contribution and sacrifice. If we only give of our abundance and never sacrifice for the kingdom of God, then we won't enjoy the rich blessings that come when we do. This requires each of us to become self-aware and assess our circumstances and determine what we could do that would raise our personal bar so that we can enjoy the subsequent blessings.

In today's dollars it is not clear how much a mite would be. However, a mite was the lowest value coinage available at that time. So, if we think about it in those terms, we can compare a mite to a penny today. Think about that. What if someone had only two pennies to their name and contributed it all to the Church or some other good cause? Or, perhaps think of it in terms of what it could provide. Say a poor person had one dollar and with that could purchase a cheap loaf of bread that would help sustain them for one meal, but instead gave it to the Church. In a relative sense, we begin to understand the level of sacrifice that the widow offered.

MARK 12:41–44

41 And Jesus sat over against the treasury, and beheld how the people cast money into the treasury: and many that were rich cast in much.

42 And there came a certain poor widow, and she threw in two mites, which make a farthing.

43 And he called unto him his disciples, and saith unto them, [Jesus] **Verily I say unto you, That this poor widow hath cast more in, than all they which have cast into the treasury:**

44 **For all they did cast in of their abundance; but she of her want did cast in all that she had, even all her living.**

LUKE 21:1–4

1 And he looked up, and saw the rich men casting their gifts into the treasury.

2 And he saw also a certain poor widow casting in thither two mites.

3 And he said, [Jesus] **Of a truth I say unto you, that this poor widow hath cast in more than they all:**

4 **For all these have of their abundance cast in unto the offerings of God: but she of her penury hath cast in all the living that she had.**

24

JESUS' LAMENT OVER JERUSALEM

MATTHEW 23:37–39; LUKE 13:34–35
Location: Near Jerusalem

Summary

While lamenting over Jerusalem, Jesus pointed out the Jews' sins, which included stoning and killing the prophets. Then He said He would have gathered them and protected them as a hen gathereth her chickens under her wings, but instead they rejected Him. Therefore, their house will be left desolate.

These are sad verses of scripture. I can picture the Savior outside of Jerusalem uttering these words. Oh, what blessings could have been theirs if only they would have seen and listened. Instead, they hardened their hearts and rejected the Savior of the world. I must ask myself, do I see, and do I listen? Is my house left desolate because I don't give my full heart to the Savior?

MATTHEW 23:37–39

37 [Jesus] O Jerusalem, Jerusalem, thou that killest the prophets, and stonest them which are sent unto thee, how often would I have gathered thy children together, even as a hen gathereth her chickens under her wings, and ye would not!

56

38 Behold, your house is left unto you desolate.

39 For I say unto you, Ye shall not see me henceforth, till ye shall say, Blessed is he that cometh in the name of the Lord.

LUKE 13:34–35

34 [Jesus] O Jerusalem, Jerusalem, which killest the prophets, and stonest them that are sent unto thee; how often would I have gathered thy children together, as a hen doth gather her brood under her wings, and ye would not!

35 Behold, your house is left unto you desolate: and verily I say unto you, Ye shall not see me, until the time come when ye shall say, Blessed is he that cometh in the name of the Lord.

25

GREEKS WISH TO
SEE JESUS

JOHN 12:20–22
Location: Jerusalem

Summary

People of Greek descent came to the Passover feast to worship as well, suggesting that these individuals had a spiritual inclination. They came to Philip asking to see Jesus, which suggests that they must have heard of Jesus and felt impressed to seek after Him.

JOHN 12:20–22

20 And there were certain Greeks among them that came up to worship at the feast:

21 The same came therefore to Philip, which was of Bethsaida of Galilee, and desired him, saying, [**Greeks**] **Sir, we would see Jesus.**

22 Philip cometh and telleth Andrew: and again Andrew and Philip tell Jesus.

26

DISCOURSE: JESUS SENT BY THE FATHER

JOHN 12:23–50
Location: Jerusalem

Summary

Finally, the time had arrived for the Savior to begin the process of the Atonement for the redemption of all mankind. He started by teaching a parable about a corn of wheat. He explained that if the corn of wheat does not fall to the ground and die, it cannot bring forth much fruit, thereby teaching that His death was necessary for the redemption of mankind. I doubt if anyone understood what He was saying and what would take place shortly.

Jesus then taught about service by saying, "He that loveth his life shall lose it; and he that hateth his life in this world shall keep it unto life eternal" (John 12:25). In other words, if we love our life we will immerse ourselves in service to God and our fellowmen and find great joy and happiness that is not found when we are self-centered and selfish. This is an interesting principle that is counterintuitive but true. He also taught that when people serve their fellow men, they are also serving the Father and will receive blessings from the Father. It is a great investment.

The Savior said His soul was troubled and asked the people if He should say, "Father, save me from this hour: but for this cause came I unto this hour." This is the first inclination that the Atonement was beginning.

The Savior was feeling the heaviness of the approaching burden that He would bear. It also appears that He was hoping that there would be another way, but He of course knew that there wouldn't be. I think that happens to us as well. Sometimes we hope there is another way, an easier way, to accomplish something, but we know in our heart that there isn't and that we must pass through it and experience the trial.

Jesus then said, "Father, glorify thy name," and the people heard a voice from heaven saying, "I have both glorified it, and will glorify it again" (John 12:28). At this, the people were astonished, and Jesus taught them that the voice was not for Him but them. The Savior taught the people that He is the light and if they come unto Him they can walk in light rather than darkness. The same applies to us today. If we come unto Christ, we will feel and experience the light and know the way.

The Gospel author noted that the Savior performed many wonderful miracles and taught powerfully, yet most still did not believe. Instead they hardened their hearts, especially the chief rulers and Pharisees. This is a telling attribute of man. We all want to be liked and to receive the praise of man. This desire sometimes causes us to shrink and not be courageous and defend the gospel because of what others may think. What can we do to seek after the will of the Lord rather than the praise of man? We must always be careful that we don't do the same as some of those who were "among the chief rulers." What a great opportunity they missed because "they loved the praise of men more than the praise of God" (John 12:43).

The Savior provided His testimony of Heavenly Father and taught us that the same characteristics and attributes that we see in Jesus are the same characteristics and attributes of the Father.

JOHN 12:23–50

23 And Jesus answered them, saying, [**Jesus**] **The hour is come, that the Son of man should be glorified.**

24 **Verily, verily, I say unto you, Except a corn of wheat fall into the ground and die, it abideth alone: but if it die, it bringeth forth much fruit.**

25 **He that loveth his life shall lose it; and he that hateth his life in this world shall keep it unto life eternal.**

26 **If any man serve me, let him follow me; and where I am, there shall also my servant be: if any man serve me, him will my Father honour.**

27 Now is my soul troubled; and what shall I say? Father, save me from this hour: but for this cause came I unto this hour.

28 Father, glorify thy name. Then came there a voice from heaven, saying, [Heavenly Father] I have both glorified it, and will glorify it again.

29 The people therefore, that stood by, and heard it, said that it thundered: others said, An angel spake to him.

30 Jesus answered and said, [Jesus] This voice came not because of me, but for your sakes.

31 Now is the judgment of this world: now shall the prince of this world be cast out.

32 And I, if I be lifted up from the earth, will draw all men unto me.

33 This he said, signifying what death he should die.

34 The people answered him, [People] We have heard out of the law that Christ abideth for ever: and how sayest thou, The Son of man must be lifted up? who is this Son of man?

35 Then Jesus said unto them, [Jesus] Yet a little while is the light with you. Walk while ye have the light, lest darkness come upon you: for he that walketh in darkness knoweth not whither he goeth.

36 While ye have light, believe in the light, that ye may be the children of light. These things spake Jesus, and departed, and did hide himself from them.

37 But though he had done so many miracles before them, yet they believed not on him:

38 That the saying of Esaias the prophet might be fulfilled, which he spake, [Esaias] Lord, who hath believed our report? and to whom hath the arm of the Lord been revealed?

39 Therefore they could not believe, because that Esaias said again,

40 [Esaias] He hath blinded their eyes, and hardened their heart; that they should not see with their eyes, nor understand with their heart, and be converted, and I should heal them.

41 These things said Esaias, when he saw his glory, and spake of him.

42 Nevertheless among the chief rulers also many believed on him; but because of the Pharisees they did not confess him, lest they should be put out of the synagogue:

43 For they loved the praise of men more than the praise of God.

44 Jesus cried and said, [**Jesus**] **He that believeth on me, believeth not on me, but on him that sent me.**

45 **And he that seeth me seeth him that sent me.**

46 **I am come a light into the world, that whosoever believeth on me should not abide in darkness.**

47 **And if any man hear my words, and believe not, I judge him not: for I came not to judge the world, but to save the world.**

48 **He that rejecteth me, and receiveth not my words, hath one that judgeth him: the word that I have spoken, the same shall judge him in the last day.**

49 **For I have not spoken of myself; but the Father which sent me, he gave me a commandment, what I should say, and what I should speak.**

50 **And I know that his commandment is life everlasting: whatsoever I speak therefore, even as the Father said unto me, so I speak.**

27

DESTRUCTION OF JERUSALEM, SIGNS OF THE SECOND COMING

MATTHEW 24; MARK 13; LUKE 21:5–38;
JOSEPH SMITH—MATTHEW 1
Location: Mount of Olives

Summary

Matthew and Mark provide an overview of the events that will take place prior to and as part of the Lord's Second Coming:

1. The temple in Jerusalem will be destroyed.
2. There will be false Christs.
3. There will be wars and rumors of wars.
4. There will be famines, pestilences, and earthquakes.
5. The disciples shall be hated and killed for the Lord's sake.
6. Many shall be offended because of the Lord and shall betray one another and hate one another.
7. Many false prophets shall arise and deceive many.
8. Iniquity shall abound, and the love of many shall wax cold.
9. The gospel shall be preached in all the world for a witness to all nations.
10. There shall be great tribulation such as not known since the beginning of the world.

11. False Christs and prophets shall arise and show great signs and wonders that may deceive the very elect.
12. The Son of Man will come from the east.
13. The sun and moon will be darkened, and the stars will fall from heaven.
14. The sign of the Son of Man shall appear in heaven, and all the tribes of the earth shall mourn. They shall see the Son of Man coming in clouds of heaven with power and great glory.
15. The Lord will send His angels with a great sound of a trumpet, and they shall gather His elect from the four winds, from one end of heaven to the other.

The gospel authors also note that the day of the Second Coming of the Lord is unknown to all but the Father. Even the angels of heaven do not know when it will take place. Therefore, we are admonished to be prepared at all times so we are not caught off guard and regret our standing before the Lord.

MATTHEW 24

1 And Jesus went out, and departed from the temple: and his disciples came to him for to shew him the buildings of the temple.

2 And Jesus said unto them, **[Jesus] See ye not all these things? verily I say unto you, There shall not be left here one stone upon another, that shall not be thrown down.**

3 And as he sat upon the mount of Olives, the disciples came unto him privately, saying, **[Disciples] Tell us, when shall these things be? and what shall be the sign of thy coming, and of the end of the world?**

4 And Jesus answered and said unto them, **[Jesus] Take heed that no man deceive you.**

5 **For many shall come in my name, saying, I am Christ; and shall deceive many.**

6 **And ye shall hear of wars and rumours of wars: see that ye be not troubled: for all these things must come to pass, but the end is not yet.**

7 **For nation shall rise against nation, and kingdom against kingdom: and there shall be famines, and pestilences, and earthquakes, in divers places.**

8 **All these are the beginning of sorrows.**

9 Then shall they deliver you up to be afflicted, and shall kill you: and ye shall be hated of all nations for my name's sake.

10 And then shall many be offended, and shall betray one another, and shall hate one another.

11 And many false prophets shall rise, and shall deceive many.

12 And because iniquity shall abound, the love of many shall wax cold.

13 But he that shall endure unto the end, the same shall be saved.

14 And this gospel of the kingdom shall be preached in all the world for a witness unto all nations; and then shall the end come.

15 When ye therefore shall see the abomination of desolation, spoken of by Daniel the prophet, stand in the holy place, (whoso readeth, let him understand:)

16 Then let them which be in Judæa flee into the mountains:

17 Let him which is on the housetop not come down to take any thing out of his house:

18 Neither let him which is in the field return back to take his clothes.

19 And woe unto them that are with child, and to them that give suck in those days!

20 But pray ye that your flight be not in the winter, neither on the sabbath day:

21 For then shall be great tribulation, such as was not since the beginning of the world to this time, no, nor ever shall be.

22 And except those days should be shortened, there should no flesh be saved: but for the elect's sake those days shall be shortened.

23 Then if any man shall say unto you, Lo, here is Christ, or there; believe it not.

24 For there shall arise false Christs, and false prophets, and shall shew great signs and wonders; insomuch that, if it were possible, they shall deceive the very elect.

25 Behold, I have told you before.

26 Wherefore if they shall say unto you, Behold, he is in the desert; go not forth: behold, he is in the secret chambers; believe it not.

27 For as the lightning cometh out of the east, and shineth even unto the west; so shall also the coming of the Son of man be.

28 For wheresoever the carcase is, there will the eagles be gathered together.

29 Immediately after the tribulation of those days shall the sun be darkened, and the moon shall not give her light, and the stars shall fall from heaven, and the powers of the heavens shall be shaken:

30 And then shall appear the sign of the Son of man in heaven: and then shall all the tribes of the earth mourn, and they shall see the Son of man coming in the clouds of heaven with power and great glory.

31 And he shall send his angels with a great sound of a trumpet, and they shall gather together his elect from the four winds, from one end of heaven to the other.

32 Now learn a parable of the fig tree; When his branch is yet tender, and putteth forth leaves, ye know that summer is nigh:

33 So likewise ye, when ye shall see all these things, know that it is near, even at the doors.

34 Verily I say unto you, This generation shall not pass, till all these things be fulfilled.

35 Heaven and earth shall pass away, but my words shall not pass away.

36 But of that day and hour knoweth no man, no, not the angels of heaven, but my Father only.

37 But as the days of Noe were, so shall also the coming of the Son of man be.

38 For as in the days that were before the flood they were eating and drinking, marrying and giving in marriage, until the day that Noe entered into the ark,

39 And knew not until the flood came, and took them all away; so shall also the coming of the Son of man be.

40 Then shall two be in the field; the one shall be taken, and the other left.

41 Two women shall be grinding at the mill; the one shall be taken, and the other left.

42 Watch therefore: for ye know not what hour your Lord doth come.

43 But know this, that if the goodman of the house had known in what watch the thief would come, he would have watched, and would not have suffered his house to be broken up.

44 Therefore be ye also ready: for in such an hour as ye think not the Son of man cometh.

45 Who then is a faithful and wise servant, whom his lord hath made ruler over his household, to give them meat in due season?

46 Blessed is that servant, whom his lord when he cometh shall find so doing.

47 Verily I say unto you, That he shall make him ruler over all his goods.

48 But and if that evil servant shall say in his heart, My lord delayeth his coming;

49 And shall begin to smite his fellow servants, and to eat and drink with the drunken;

50 The lord of that servant shall come in a day when he looketh not for him, and in an hour that he is not aware of,

51 And shall cut him asunder, and appoint him his portion with the hypocrites: there shall be weeping and gnashing of teeth.

MARK 13

1 And as he went out of the temple, one of his disciples saith unto him, [Disciples] **Master, see what manner of stones and what buildings are here!**

2 And Jesus answering said unto him, [Jesus] **Seest thou these great buildings? there shall not be left one stone upon another, that shall not be thrown down.**

3 And as he sat upon the mount of Olives over against the temple, Peter and James and John and Andrew asked him privately,

4 [Peter, James, John, and Andrew] Tell us, when shall these things be? and what shall be the sign when all these things shall be fulfilled?

5 And Jesus answering them began to say, [Jesus] Take heed lest any man deceive you:

6 For many shall come in my name, saying, I am Christ; and shall deceive many.

7 And when ye shall hear of wars and rumours of wars, be ye not troubled: for such things must needs be; but the end shall not be yet.

8 For nation shall rise against nation, and kingdom against kingdom: and there shall be earthquakes in divers places, and there shall be famines and troubles: these are the beginnings of sorrows.

9 But take heed to yourselves: for they shall deliver you up to councils; and in the synagogues ye shall be beaten: and ye shall be brought before rulers and kings for my sake, for a testimony against them.

10 And the gospel must first be published among all nations.

11 But when they shall lead you, and deliver you up, take no thought beforehand what ye shall speak, neither do ye premeditate: but whatsoever shall be given you in that hour, that speak ye: for it is not ye that speak, but the Holy Ghost.

12 Now the brother shall betray the brother to death, and the father the son; and children shall rise up against their parents, and shall cause them to be put to death.

13 And ye shall be hated of all men for my name's sake: but he that shall endure unto the end, the same shall be saved.

14 But when ye shall see the abomination of desolation, spoken of by Daniel the prophet, standing where it ought not, (let him that readeth understand,) then let them that be in Judæa flee to the mountains:

15 And let him that is on the housetop not go down into the house, neither enter therein, to take any thing out of his house:

16 And let him that is in the field not turn back again for to take up his garment.

17 But woe to them that are with child, and to them that give suck in those days!

18 And pray ye that your flight be not in the winter.

19 For in those days shall be affliction, such as was not from the beginning of the creation which God created unto this time, neither shall be.

20 And except that the Lord had shortened those days, no flesh should be saved: but for the elect's sake, whom he hath chosen, he hath shortened the days.

21 And then if any man shall say to you, Lo, here is Christ; or, lo, he is there; believe him not:

22 For false Christs and false prophets shall rise, and shall shew signs and wonders, to seduce, if it were possible, even the elect.

23 But take ye heed: behold, I have foretold you all things.

24 But in those days, after that tribulation, the sun shall be darkened, and the moon shall not give her light,

25 And the stars of heaven shall fall, and the powers that are in heaven shall be shaken.

26 And then shall they see the Son of man coming in the clouds with great power and glory.

27 And then shall he send his angels, and shall gather together his elect from the four winds, from the uttermost part of the earth to the uttermost part of heaven.

28 Now learn a parable of the fig tree; When her branch is yet tender, and putteth forth leaves, ye know that summer is near:

29 So ye in like manner, when ye shall see these things come to pass, know that it is nigh, even at the doors.

30 Verily I say unto you, that this generation shall not pass, till all these things be done.

31 Heaven and earth shall pass away: but my words shall not pass away.

32 But of that day and that hour knoweth no man, no, not the angels which are in heaven, neither the Son, but the Father.

33 Take ye heed, watch and pray: for ye know not when the time is.

34 For the Son of man is as a man taking a far journey, who left his house, and gave authority to his servants, and to every man his work, and commanded the porter to watch.

35 Watch ye therefore: for ye know not when the master of the house cometh, at even, or at midnight, or at the cock crowing, or in the morning:

36 Lest coming suddenly he find you sleeping.

37 And what I say unto you I say unto all, Watch.

LUKE 21:5–38

5 And as some spake of the temple, how it was adorned with goodly stones and gifts, he said,

6 [Jesus] As for these things which ye behold, the days will come, in the which there shall not be left one stone upon another, that shall not be thrown down.

7 And they asked him, saying, Master, but when shall these things be? and what sign will there be when these things shall come to pass?

8 And he said, [Jesus] Take heed that ye be not deceived: for many shall come in my name, saying, I am Christ; and the time draweth near: go ye not therefore after them.

9 But when ye shall hear of wars and commotions, be not terrified: for these things must first come to pass; but the end is not by and by.

10 Then said he unto them, Nation shall rise against nation, and kingdom against kingdom:

11 And great earthquakes shall be in divers places, and famines, and pestilences; and fearful sights and great signs shall there be from heaven.

12 But before all these, they shall lay their hands on you, and persecute you, delivering you up to the

synagogues, and into prisons, being brought before kings and rulers for my name's sake.

13 And it shall turn to you for a testimony.

14 Settle it therefore in your hearts, not to meditate before what ye shall answer:

15 For I will give you a mouth and wisdom, which all your adversaries shall not be able to gainsay nor resist.

16 And ye shall be betrayed both by parents, and brethren, and kinsfolks, and friends; and some of you shall they cause to be put to death.

17 And ye shall be hated of all men for my name's sake.

18 But there shall not an hair of your head perish.

19 In your patience possess ye your souls.

20 And when ye shall see Jerusalem compassed with armies, then know that the desolation thereof is nigh.

21 Then let them which are in Judæa flee to the mountains; and let them which are in the midst of it depart out; and let not them that are in the countries enter thereinto.

22 For these be the days of vengeance, that all things which are written may be fulfilled.

23 But woe unto them that are with child, and to them that give suck, in those days! for there shall be great distress in the land, and wrath upon this people.

24 And they shall fall by the edge of the sword, and shall be led away captive into all nations: and Jerusalem shall be trodden down of the Gentiles, until the times of the Gentiles be fulfilled.

25 And there shall be signs in the sun, and in the moon, and in the stars; and upon the earth distress of nations, with perplexity; the sea and the waves roaring;

26 Men's hearts failing them for fear, and for looking after those things which are coming on the earth: for the powers of heaven shall be shaken.

27 And then shall they see the Son of man coming in a cloud with power and great glory.

28 And when these things begin to come to pass, then look up, and lift up your heads; for your redemption draweth nigh.

29 And he spake to them a parable; Behold the fig tree, and all the trees;

30 When they now shoot forth, ye see and know of your own selves that summer is now nigh at hand.

31 So likewise ye, when ye see these things come to pass, know ye that the kingdom of God is nigh at hand.

32 Verily I say unto you, This generation shall not pass away, till all be fulfilled.

33 Heaven and earth shall pass away: but my words shall not pass away.

34 And take heed to yourselves, lest at any time your hearts be overcharged with surfeiting, and drunkenness, and cares of this life, and so that day come upon you unawares.

35 For as a snare shall it come on all them that dwell on the face of the whole earth.

36 Watch ye therefore, and pray always, that ye may be accounted worthy to escape all these things that shall come to pass, and to stand before the Son of man.

37 And in the day time he was teaching in the temple; and at night he went out, and abode in the mount that is called the mount of Olives.

38 And all the people came early in the morning to him in the temple, for to hear him.

JST, LUKE 21:24–26.

Compare Luke 21:25–26.

Jesus speaks of some signs of His coming.

24 Now these things he spake unto them, concerning the destruction of Jerusalem. And then his disciples asked him, saying, [Disciples] Master, tell us concerning thy coming?

25 And he answered them, and said, [Jesus] In the generation in which the times of the Gentiles shall be fulfilled, there shall be signs in the sun, and in the

moon, and in the stars; and upon the earth distress of nations with perplexity, like the sea and the waves roaring. The earth also shall be troubled, and the waters of the great deep;

26 Men's hearts failing them for fear, and for looking after those things which are coming on the earth. For the powers of heaven shall be shaken.

JST, LUKE 21:32.

Compare Luke 21:32.
All will be fulfilled when the times of the Gentiles are fulfilled.

32 [Jesus] Verily I say unto you, this generation, the generation when the times of the Gentiles be fulfilled, shall not pass away till all be fulfilled.

JOSEPH SMITH—MATTHEW 1

(An extract from the translation of the Bible as revealed to Joseph Smith the Prophet in 1831: Matthew 23:39 and chapter 24.)

1 [Jesus] For I say unto you, that ye shall not see me henceforth and know that I am he of whom it is written by the prophets, until ye shall say: Blessed is he who cometh in the name of the Lord, in the clouds of heaven, and all the holy angels with him. Then understood his disciples that he should come again on the earth, after that he was glorified and crowned on the right hand of God.

2 And Jesus went out, and departed from the temple; and his disciples came to him, for to hear him, saying: [Disciples] Master, show us concerning the buildings of the temple, as thou hast said—They shall be thrown down, and left unto you desolate.

3 And Jesus said unto them: [Jesus] See ye not all these things, and do ye not understand them? Verily I say unto you, there shall not be left here, upon this temple, one stone upon another that shall not be thrown down.

4 And Jesus left them, and went upon the Mount of Olives. And as he sat upon the Mount of Olives, the disciples came unto him privately, saying: [Disciples] Tell us when shall these things be which thou hast said concerning the

destruction of the temple, and the Jews; and what is the sign of thy coming, and of the end of the world, or the destruction of the wicked, which is the end of the world?

5 And Jesus answered, and said unto them: [Jesus] Take heed that no man deceive you;

6 For many shall come in my name, saying—I am Christ—and shall deceive many;

7 Then shall they deliver you up to be afflicted, and shall kill you, and ye shall be hated of all nations, for my name's sake;

8 And then shall many be offended, and shall betray one another, and shall hate one another;

9 And many false prophets shall arise, and shall deceive many;

10 And because iniquity shall abound, the love of many shall wax cold;

11 But he that remaineth steadfast and is not overcome, the same shall be saved.

12 When you, therefore, shall see the abomination of desolation, spoken of by Daniel the prophet, concerning the destruction of Jerusalem, then you shall stand in the holy place; whoso readeth let him understand.

13 Then let them who are in Judea flee into the mountains;

14 Let him who is on the housetop flee, and not return to take anything out of his house;

15 Neither let him who is in the field return back to take his clothes;

16 And wo unto them that are with child, and unto them that give suck in those days;

17 Therefore, pray ye the Lord that your flight be not in the winter, neither on the Sabbath day;

18 For then, in those days, shall be great tribulation on the Jews, and upon the inhabitants of Jerusalem, such as was not before sent upon Israel, of God, since the beginning of their kingdom until this time; no, nor ever shall be sent again upon Israel.

19 All things which have befallen them are only the beginning of the sorrows which shall come upon them.

20 And except those days should be shortened, there should none of their flesh be saved; but for the elect's sake, according to the covenant, those days shall be shortened.

21 Behold, these things I have spoken unto you concerning the Jews; and again, after the tribulation of those days which shall come upon Jerusalem, if any man shall say unto you, Lo, here is Christ, or there, believe him not;

22 For in those days there shall also arise false Christs, and false prophets, and shall show great signs and wonders, insomuch, that, if possible, they shall deceive the very elect, who are the elect according to the covenant.

23 Behold, I speak these things unto you for the elect's sake; and you also shall hear of wars, and rumors of wars; see that ye be not troubled, for all I have told you must come to pass; but the end is not yet.

24 Behold, I have told you before;

25 Wherefore, if they shall say unto you: Behold, he is in the desert; go not forth: Behold, he is in the secret chambers; believe it not;

26 For as the light of the morning cometh out of the east, and shineth even unto the west, and covereth the whole earth, so shall also the coming of the Son of Man be.

27 And now I show unto you a parable. Behold, wheresoever the carcass is, there will the eagles be gathered together; so likewise shall mine elect be gathered from the four quarters of the earth.

28 And they shall hear of wars, and rumors of wars.

29 Behold I speak for mine elect's sake; for nation shall rise against nation, and kingdom against kingdom; there shall be famines, and pestilences, and earthquakes, in divers places.

30 And again, because iniquity shall abound, the love of men shall wax cold; but he that shall not be overcome, the same shall be saved.

31 And again, this Gospel of the Kingdom shall be preached in all the world, for a witness unto all nations,

and then shall the end come, or the destruction of the wicked;

32 And again shall the abomination of desolation, spoken of by Daniel the prophet, be fulfilled.

33 And immediately after the tribulation of those days, the sun shall be darkened, and the moon shall not give her light, and the stars shall fall from heaven, and the powers of heaven shall be shaken.

34 Verily, I say unto you, this generation, in which these things shall be shown forth, shall not pass away until all I have told you shall be fulfilled.

35 Although, the days will come, that heaven and earth shall pass away; yet my words shall not pass away, but all shall be fulfilled.

36 And, as I said before, after the tribulation of those days, and the powers of the heavens shall be shaken, then shall appear the sign of the Son of Man in heaven, and then shall all the tribes of the earth mourn; and they shall see the Son of Man coming in the clouds of heaven, with power and great glory;

37 And whoso treasureth up my word, shall not be deceived, for the Son of Man shall come, and he shall send his angels before him with the great sound of a trumpet, and they shall gather together the remainder of his elect from the four winds, from one end of heaven to the other.

38 Now learn a parable of the fig tree—When its branches are yet tender, and it begins to put forth leaves, you know that summer is nigh at hand;

39 So likewise, mine elect, when they shall see all these things, they shall know that he is near, even at the doors;

40 But of that day, and hour, no one knoweth; no, not the angels of God in heaven, but my Father only.

41 But as it was in the days of Noah, so it shall be also at the coming of the Son of Man;

42 For it shall be with them, as it was in the days which were before the flood; for until the day that Noah

entered into the ark they were eating and drinking, marrying and giving in marriage;

43 And knew not until the flood came, and took them all away; so shall also the coming of the Son of Man be.

44 Then shall be fulfilled that which is written, that in the last days, two shall be in the field, the one shall be taken, and the other left;

45 Two shall be grinding at the mill, the one shall be taken, and the other left;

46 And what I say unto one, I say unto all men; watch, therefore, for you know not at what hour your Lord doth come.

47 But know this, if the good man of the house had known in what watch the thief would come, he would have watched, and would not have suffered his house to have been broken up, but would have been ready.

48 Therefore be ye also ready, for in such an hour as ye think not, the Son of Man cometh.

49 Who, then, is a faithful and wise servant, whom his lord hath made ruler over his household, to give them meat in due season?

50 Blessed is that servant whom his lord, when he cometh, shall find so doing; and verily I say unto you, he shall make him ruler over all his goods.

51 But if that evil servant shall say in his heart: My lord delayeth his coming,

52 And shall begin to smite his fellow-servants, and to eat and drink with the drunken,

53 The lord of that servant shall come in a day when he looketh not for him, and in an hour that he is not aware of,

54 And shall cut him asunder, and shall appoint him his portion with the hypocrites; there shall be weeping and gnashing of teeth.

55 And thus cometh the end of the wicked, according to the prophecy of Moses, saying: They shall be cut off from among the people; but the end of the earth is not yet, but by and by.

28

PARABLE: TEN VIRGINS

MATTHEW 25:1–13; LUKE 12:35–36; D&C 45:56–59
Location: Mount of Olives

Summary

The parable of the ten virgins teaches us the importance of preparation, especially spiritual preparation, so that we are always ready to meet the Savior. In this parable, the Savior likens the kingdom of heaven to ten virgins, who went forth with their lamps to meet the bridegroom. Five of the virgins were wise and took extra oil for their lamps, but five were foolish and did not. The bridegroom was late to the wedding, so the virgins slept. At midnight, when it was announced that the bridegroom was coming, the virgins arose and trimmed their lamps. The lamps of the foolish had no oil. The foolish virgins then asked the wise virgins if they could borrow some of theirs, but the wise virgins answered that they had only enough for themselves. They encouraged the foolish virgins to go to those who sell oil and try to buy more. While the foolish virgins were away trying to buy oil, the bridegroom came. The wise virgins went into the house with him and he closed the door. When the foolish virgins returned, they asked the Lord to let them in, but he said, "I know you not." The oil represents the Holy Ghost that lights the way for the Saints,[32] and Jesus encouraged his disciples to always be prepared, for "ye know neither the day nor the hour wherein the Son of man cometh."

Referring to the parable of the ten virgins, Elder Marvin J. Ashton said,

It can be properly and appropriately concluded that the ten virgins represent the people of the Church of Jesus Christ, and not alone the rank and file of the world. The wise and foolish virgins, all of them, had been invited to the wedding supper; they had knowledge of the importance of the occasion. They were not pagans, heathens, or gentiles, nor were they known as corrupt or lost, but rather they were informed people who had the saving, exalting gospel in their possession, but had not made it the center of their lives. They knew the way, but were foolishly unprepared for the coming of the bridegroom. All, even the foolish ones, trimmed their lamps at his coming, but their oil was used up. In the most needed moment there was none available to refill their lamps. All had been warned their entire lives."[33]

President Wilford Woodruff said,

Now the question is, how can we keep oil in our lamps? By keeping the commandments of God, remembering our prayers, doing as we are told by the revelations of Jesus Christ, and otherwise assisting in building up Zion. When we are laboring for the kingdom of God, we will have oil in our lamps, our light will shine, and we will feel the testimony of the Spirit of God. On the other hand, if we set our hearts upon the things of the world and seek for the honors of men, we shall walk in the dark and not in the light. If we don't value our priesthood, and the work of this priesthood, the building up of the kingdom of God, the rearing of temples, the redeeming of our dead, and the carrying out of the great work unto which we have been ordained by the God of Israel—if we do not feel that these things are more valuable to us than the things of the world, we will have no oil in our lamps, no light, and we shall fail to be present at the marriage supper of the Lamb."[34]

MATTHEW 25:1–13

1 [Jesus] Then shall the kingdom of heaven be likened unto ten virgins, which took their lamps, and went forth to meet the bridegroom.

2 And five of them were wise, and five were foolish.

3 They that were foolish took their lamps, and took no oil with them:

4 But the wise took oil in their vessels with their lamps.

5 While the bridegroom tarried, they all slumbered and slept.

6 And at midnight there was a cry made, Behold, the bridegroom cometh; go ye out to meet him.

7 Then all those virgins arose, and trimmed their lamps.

8 And the foolish said unto the wise, Give us of your oil; for our lamps are gone out.

9 But the wise answered, saying, Not so; lest there be not enough for us and you: but go ye rather to them that sell, and buy for yourselves.

10 And while they went to buy, the bridegroom came; and they that were ready went in with him to the marriage: and the door was shut.

11 Afterward came also the other virgins, saying, Lord, Lord, open to us.

12 But he answered and said, Verily I say unto you, I know you not.

13 Watch therefore, for ye know neither the day nor the hour wherein the Son of man cometh.

29

PARABLE: TALENTS

MATTHEW 25:14–30
Location: Mount of Olives

Summary

The parable of the talents[35] provides insight into how the Lord thinks about our responsibilities and future rewards. Jesus begins the parable by pointing out that a man who had three servants was getting ready to travel into a far country and would be away for quite some time. The man had eight talents (precious metal pieces that represented units of value) that he wanted his servants to invest while he was gone so that his wealth would grow in his absence. After assessing the servants' abilities, he gave five talents to one servant, two talents to a second servant, and one talent to a third servant. He charged them to go to work to increase the value of that which he gave them.

While the lord of the house was gone, the servant with five talents worked hard and doubled his talents to ten. The servants with two talents also worked hard and doubled his talents to four. However, the servant with one talent was afraid of losing it, so he buried it in the earth and waited for the return of his lord. When the lord of the house returned and found that two of the servants had doubled their talents, he said to each of them, "Well done, thou good and faithful servant: thou hast been faithful over a few things, I will make thee ruler over many things: enter thou into the joy of

81

the lord" (Matthew 25:21). The lord was not pleased with the servant who had buried his one talent. When asked why he buried it, the servant said that he was afraid, so he buried it in the earth. At this response, the lord took the talent and gave it to the servant who had ten talents and commanded that the unprofitable servant be cast out.

We can learn many lessons from this parable, but perhaps the obvious one is that the Lord expects us to work hard with the gifts and talents He has given us to build His Kingdom and be profitable servants. Each of us has different gifts and talents, but if we increase the talents that the Lord has given us individually, even though they may be fewer than those given to another person, our reward will be the same. If, however, we do nothing with our talents to help build the kingdom, we will be cast out and have no reward.

MATTHEW 25:14–30

14 [Jesus]For the kingdom of heaven is as a man travelling into a far country, who called his own servants, and delivered unto them his goods.

15 And unto one he gave five talents, to another two, and to another one; to every man according to his several ability; and straightway took his journey.

16 Then he that had received the five talents went and traded with the same, and made them other five talents.

17 And likewise he that had received two, he also gained other two.

18 But he that had received one went and digged in the earth, and hid his lord's money.

19 After a long time the lord of those servants cometh, and reckoneth with them.

20 And so he that had received five talents came and brought other five talents, saying, Lord, thou deliveredst unto me five talents: behold, I have gained beside them five talents more.

21 His lord said unto him, Well done, thou good and faithful servant: thou hast been faithful over a few things, I will make thee ruler over many things: enter thou into the joy of thy lord.

22 He also that had received two talents came and said, Lord, thou deliveredst unto me two talents: behold, I have gained two other talents beside them.

23 His lord said unto him, Well done, good and faithful servant; thou hast been faithful over a few things, I will make thee ruler over many things: enter thou into the joy of thy lord.

24 Then he which had received the one talent came and said, Lord, I knew thee that thou art an hard man, reaping where thou hast not sown, and gathering where thou hast not strawed:

25 And I was afraid, and went and hid thy talent in the earth: lo, there thou hast that is thine.

26 His lord answered and said unto him, Thou wicked and slothful servant, thou knewest that I reap where I sowed not, and gather where I have not strawed:

27 Thou oughtest therefore to have put my money to the exchangers, and then at my coming I should have received mine own with usury.

28 Take therefore the talent from him, and give it unto him which hath ten talents.

29 For unto every one that hath shall be given, and he shall have abundance: but from him that hath not shall be taken away even that which he hath.

30 And cast ye the unprofitable servant into outer darkness: there shall be weeping and gnashing of teeth.

30

PARABLE: SHEEP, GOATS

MATTHEW 25:31–46
Location: Mount of Olives

Summary

The parable of the talents teaches us the importance of being profitable servants by actively using the gifts and talents the Lord has given us to build His Kingdom, whereas the parable of the sheep and the goats gives us more insight into the specific things that we can do to make us more profitable servants. In the verses that follow, we get a sense that serving others, especially those who are less advantaged or those who are struggling, is a high priority to the Lord. The Lord makes it clear that when we are serving our fellowman we are serving Him.

MATTHEW 25:31–46

31 [Jesus] When the Son of man shall come in his glory, and all the holy angels with him, then shall he sit upon the throne of his glory:

32 And before him shall be gathered all nations: and he shall separate them one from another, as a shepherd divideth his sheep from the goats:

33 And he shall set the sheep on his right hand, but the goats on the left.

34 Then shall the King say unto them on his right hand, Come, ye blessed of my Father, inherit the kingdom prepared for you from the foundation of the world:

35 For I was an hungred, and ye gave me meat: I was thirsty, and ye gave me drink: I was a stranger, and ye took me in:

36 Naked, and ye clothed me: I was sick, and ye visited me: I was in prison, and ye came unto me.

37 Then shall the righteous answer him, saying, Lord, when saw we thee an hungred, and fed thee? or thirsty, and gave thee drink?

38 When saw we thee a stranger, and took thee in? or naked, and clothed thee?

39 Or when saw we thee sick, or in prison, and came unto thee?

40 And the King shall answer and say unto them, Verily I say unto you, Inasmuch as ye have done it unto one of the least of these my brethren, ye have done it unto me.

41 Then shall he say also unto them on the left hand, Depart from me, ye cursed, into everlasting fire, prepared for the devil and his angels:

42 For I was an hungred, and ye gave me no meat: I was thirsty, and ye gave me no drink:

43 I was a stranger, and ye took me not in: naked, and ye clothed me not: sick, and in prison, and ye visited me not.

44 Then shall they also answer him, saying, Lord, when saw we thee an hungred, or athirst, or a stranger, or naked, or sick, or in prison, and did not minister unto thee?

45 Then shall he answer them, saying, Verily I say unto you, Inasmuch as ye did it not to one of the least of these, ye did it not to me.

46 And these shall go away into everlasting punishment: but the righteous into life eternal.

31

THE LAST DAY BEFORE PASSOVER

MATTHEW 26:2; MARK 14:1
Location: Unknown

Summary

The Lord forewarns the disciples of His impending betrayal and death by crucifixion. Mark points out that right before the feast of the Passover the chief priests and scribes were seriously conspiring on how they would murder Jesus. What an incredible thing, that men who were deemed spiritual leaders in their community would develop such great hatred and animosity toward someone who had performed such wonderful miracles and taught such great doctrine. These verses give us some insight into the detrimental nature of pride and how it can lead to catastrophic consequences.

MATTHEW 26:2

2 [Jesus] **Ye know that after two days is the feast of the passover, and the Son of man is betrayed to be crucified.**[36]

MARK 14:1

1 After two days was the feast of the passover, and of unleavened bread: and the chief priests and the scribes sought how they might take him by craft, and put him to death.

32

JESUS' PROPHECY OF THE CRUCIFIXION

MATTHEW 26:1–2
Location: Near Jerusalem

Summary

The Savior knew that He was going to be put to death and die at the hands of the Jews. He also knew exactly how it was going to happen. This knowledge had to be a very heavy burden to carry. The natural man would be terrified by such knowledge, yet there is every indication that Jesus was at peace during this time.

MATTHEW 26:1–2

1 And it came to pass, when Jesus had finished all these sayings, he said unto his disciples,

2 [Jesus] Ye know that after two days is the feast of the passover, and the Son of man is betrayed to be crucified.

33

CONSPIRACY AT CAIAPHAS'S PALACE

MATTHEW 26:3–5; MARK 14:1–2; LUKE 22:1–2
Location: Jerusalem

Summary

The Feast of the Passover is also the Feast of Unleavened Bread. The chief priests, scribes, and elders wanted to find an opportunity to kidnap Jesus secretly and then kill him. They were concerned that the people who loved Him would create an uproar, so they conspired to wait until after the feast; therefore, it is clear that the conspiracy included cold-blooded murder.

MATTHEW 26:3–5

3 Then assembled together the chief priests, and the scribes, and the elders of the people, unto the palace of the high priest, who was called Caiaphas,

4 And consulted that they might take Jesus by subtilty, and kill him.

5 But they said, [**Chief Priests, Scribes, and Elders**] **Not on the feast day, lest there be an uproar among the people.**

MARK 14:1–2

1 After two days was the feast of the passover, and of unleavened bread: and the chief priests and the scribes sought how they might take him by craft, and put him to death.

2 But they said, [**Chief Priests, Scribes, and Elders**] **Not on the feast day, lest there be an uproar of the people.**

LUKE 22:1–2

1 Now the feast of unleavened bread drew nigh, which is called the Passover.

2 And the chief priests and scribes sought how they might kill him; for they feared the people.

34

JUDAS'S CONSPIRACY TO BETRAY JESUS

MATTHEW 26:14–16; MARK 14:10–11;
LUKE 22:3–6
Location: Jerusalem

Summary

Satan put it into the heart of Judas to betray the Savior. Afterward, Judas[37] sought out the chief priests who were glad to enter into a secret covenant with him. The chief priests offered to pay Judas thirty pieces of silver if he would deliver the Lord to them so that they could kill Him. This was a coordinated effort between Judas and the chief priests to murder the Savior. How sad it is that Judas, one of the Twelve Apostles, would allow Satan to get such great hold on his heart. This example is a lesson to each of us that if we are not always on our guard, Satan may get a great hold on us and tempt us to do things that would be everlastingly hurtful and lead to our condemnation. I wonder what the principle driver was that caused Judas to commit such an act. Was it greed? Was it power? Was it animosity toward the Lord for some reason? Perhaps it was all of the above.

MATTHEW 26:14–16

14 Then one of the twelve, called Judas Iscariot, went unto the chief priests,

15 And said unto them, [**Judas Iscariot**] **What will ye give me, and I will deliver him unto you?** And they covenanted with him for thirty pieces of silver.

16 And from that time he sought opportunity to betray him.

MARK 14:10–11

10 And Judas Iscariot, one of the twelve, went unto the chief priests, to betray him unto them.

11 And when they heard it, they were glad, and promised to give him money. And he sought how he might conveniently betray him.

LUKE 22:3–6

3 Then entered Satan into Judas surnamed Iscariot, being of the number of the twelve.

4 And he went his way, and communed with the chief priests and captains, how he might betray him unto them.

5 And they were glad, and covenanted to give him money.

6 And he promised, and sought opportunity to betray him unto them in the absence of the multitude.

35

THE FIRST DAY OF
UNLEAVENED BREAD

MATTHEW 26:17–19; MARK 14:12–16;
LUKE 22:7–13
Location: Jerusalem

Summary

As the day of unleavened bread, or the Passover, had arrived, the disciples asked the Savior where they would go to eat the Passover meal. The Savior told Peter and John to go into the city and there they would find a man bearing a pitcher of water. They were to follow him into the house and say unto the "goodman" of the house, "Where is the guest chamber, where I shall eat the Passover with my disciples?" (Mark 14:14). The Lord told them that they would be shown a large, furnished upper room where they could prepare for the Passover meal.

MATTHEW 26:17–19

17 Now the first day of the feast of unleavened bread the disciples came to Jesus, saying unto him, [**Disciples**] **Where wilt thou that we prepare for thee to eat the passover?**

18 And he said, [**Jesus**] **Go into the city to such a man, and say unto him, The Master saith, My time is at hand; I will keep the passover at thy house with my disciples.**

19 And the disciples did as Jesus had appointed them; and they made ready the passover.

MARK 14:12–16

12 And the first day of unleavened bread, when they killed the passover, his disciples said unto him, [**Disciples**] **Where wilt thou that we go and prepare that thou mayest eat the passover?**

13 And he sendeth forth two of his disciples, and saith unto them, [**Jesus**] **Go ye into the city, and there shall meet you a man bearing a pitcher of water: follow him.**

14 **And wheresoever he shall go in, say ye to the goodman of the house, The Master saith, Where is the guestchamber, where I shall eat the passover with my disciples?**

15 **And he will shew you a large upper room furnished and prepared: there make ready for us.**

16 And his disciples went forth, and came into the city, and found as he had said unto them: and they made ready the passover.

LUKE 22:7–13

7 Then came the day of unleavened bread, when the passover must be killed.

8 And he sent Peter and John, saying, [**Jesus**] **Go and prepare us the passover, that we may eat.**

9 And they said unto him, [**Peter and John**] **Where wilt thou that we prepare?**

10 And he said unto them, [**Jesus**] **Behold, when ye are entered into the city, there shall a man meet you, bearing a pitcher of water; follow him into the house where he entereth in.**

11 **And ye shall say unto the goodman of the house, The Master saith unto thee, Where is the guestchamber, where I shall eat the passover with my disciples?**

12 **And he shall shew you a large upper room furnished: there make ready.**

13 And they went, and found as he had said unto them: and they made ready the passover.

36

THE LAST SUPPER BEGINS

MATTHEW 26:20; MARK 14:17;
LUKE 22:13–14; JOHN 13:1–2
Location: Jerusalem

Summary

In the evening the Lord sat down to have the Passover meal with His Twelve Apostles. John notes that the Lord loved His brethren of the Twelve unto the end. John also notes that Satan was the one who put it in the heart of Judas Iscariot to betray the Lord.

> **MATTHEW 26:20**
>
> 20 Now when the even was come, he sat down with the twelve.

> **MARK 14:17**
>
> 17 And in the evening he cometh with the twelve.

> **LUKE 22:13–14**
>
> 13 And they went, and found as he had said unto them: and they made ready the passover.
>
> 14 And when the hour was come, he sat down, and the twelve apostles with him.

JOHN 13:1–2

1 Now before the feast of the passover, when Jesus knew that his hour was come that he should depart out of this world unto the Father, having loved his own which were in the world, he loved them unto the end.

2 And supper being ended, the devil having now put into the heart of Judas Iscariot, Simon's son, to betray him.

37

STRIFE OVER GREATNESS

LUKE 22:24–30
Location: Jerusalem

Summary

During the Passover meal, the Apostles argued a little regarding rank and status. The Savior taught them about serving each other and said that He serveth them as an example. This tendency to point out self-importance is inherent in all of us. We must check ourselves continually and make sure we don't fall into that trap.

LUKE 22:24–30

24 And there was also a strife among them, which of them should be accounted the greatest.

25 And he said unto them, [**Jesus**] **the kings of the Gentiles exercise lordship over them; and they that exercise authority upon them are called benefactors.**

26 **But ye shall not be so: but he that is greatest among you, let him be as the younger; and he that is chief, as he that doth serve.**

27 **For whether is greater, he that sitteth at meat, or he that serveth? Is not he that sitteth at meat? But I am among you as he that serveth.**

28 Ye are they which have continued with me in my temptations.

29 And I appoint unto you a kingdom, as my Father hath appointed unto me;

30 That ye may eat and drink at my table in my kingdom, and sit on thrones judging the twelve tribes of Israel.

38

JESUS WASHES DISCIPLES' FEET

JOHN 13:2–5
Location: Jerusalem

Summary

At the conclusion of the supper, the Savior removed His robes and began to wash the disciples' feet. The symbolism of this act is powerful. The Savior bowed beneath His brethren of the Twelve to serve them. He did not rule over them with worldly superiority but wanted to help them. That example is powerful for us as well. We are not "over" anyone; we are the servant to all.

JOHN 13:2–5

2 And supper being ended, the devil having now put into the heart of Judas Iscariot, Simon's son, to betray him;

3 Jesus knowing that the Father had given all things into his hands, and that he was come from God, and went to God;

4 He riseth from supper, and laid aside his garments; and took a towel, and girded himself.

5 After that he poureth water into a basin, and began to wash the disciples' fee, and to wipe the with the towel wherewith he was girded.

39

PETER'S PROTEST

JOHN 13:6–12
Location: Jerusalem

Summary

When the Savior began to wash the disciples' feet, Peter protested by saying that he should wash the Savior's feet, not the other way around. The Savior pointed out that if Peter did not allow the Savior to wash his feet, he would have no part with the Lord. At this Peter said, "Not my feet only, but also my hands and my head" (John 13:9).

JOHN 13:6–12

6 Then cometh he to Simon Peter: and Peter saith unto him, [**Peter**] **Lord, dost thou wash my feet?**

7 Jesus answered and said unto him, [**Jesus**] **What I do thou knowest not now, but thou shalt know hearafter.**

8 Peter saith unto him, [**Peter**] **Thou shalt never wash my feet.** Jesus answered him, [**Jesus**] **If I was thee not, thou hast no part with me.**

9 Simon Peter saith unto him, [**Peter**] **Lord, not my feet only, but also my hands and my head.**

10 Jesus saith to him, [Jesus] He that is washed need-eth not save to wash his feet, but is clean every whit: and ye are clean, but not all.

11 For he knew who should betray him; therefore said he, [Jesus] Ye are not all clean.

12 So after he had washed their feet, and had taken his garments, and was set down again, he said unto them, [Jesus] Know ye what I have done to you?

JST, JOHN 13:8–10.
Compare John 13:8–10.
Jesus washes the feet of the Apostles to fulfill the law of the Jews.

8 Peter saith unto him, [Peter] Thou needest not to wash my feet. Jesus answered him, [Jesus] If I wash thee not, thou hast no part with me.

9 Simon Peter saith unto him, [Peter] Lord, not my feet only, but also my hands and my head.

10 Jesus saith to him, [Jesus] He that has washed his hands and his head, needeth not save to wash his feet, but is clean every whit; and ye are clean, but not all. Now this was the custom of the Jews under their law; wherefore, Jesus did this that the law might be fulfilled.

40

JESUS' EXAMPLE

JOHN 13:13–17
Location: Jerusalem

Summary

The Savior taught an important principle about service in His kingdom. We are never to lord over others in any way but be the servant of all. By washing His disciples' feet, Jesus provided an example for them. He taught them that if they learn and internalize this principle of service that they would be happy, suggesting that if we remember and internalize this principle we will also find joy.

JOHN 13:13–17

13 [Jesus] Ye call me Master and Lord: and ye say well; for so I am.

14 If I then, your Lord and Master, have washed your feet; ye also ought to wash one another's feet.

15 For I have given you an example, that ye should do as I have done to you.

16 Verily, verily, I say unto you, The servant is not greater than his lord; neigh he that is sent greater than he that sent him.

17 If ye know these things, happy are ye if ye do them.

41

"ONE OF YOU SHALL BETRAY ME"

MATTHEW 26:21–25; MARK 14:18–21;
LUKE 22:21–23; JOHN 13:18–30
Location: Jerusalem

Summary

During the supper, Jesus pointed out that one of the Twelve would betray Him. It appears that this caused quite a discussion, and some asked if it was them. There is some ambiguity as to what happens next. Three of the Gospel writers indicate that the Lord said that He who dipped His bread with Him was the one, while one Gospel writer says that the Lord would dip His bread and give it to the person who would betray Him. It appears that although the Savior and Judas knew who would betray Him, the other eleven didn't know nor pick up on the cues as to who the betrayer was. What is clear, however, is that in the end, the Lord knew who His betrayer was and dismissed him to go and carry out his plan.

MATTHEW 26:21–25

21 And as they did eat, he said, [**Jesus**] **Verily I say unto you, that one of you shall betray me.**

22 And they were exceeding sorrowful, and began every one of them to say unto him, [**Disciples**] **Lord, is it I?**

23 And he answered and said, [Jesus] He that dippeth his hand with me in the dish, the same shall betray me.

24 The Son of man goeth as it is written of him: but woe unto that man by whom the Son of man is betrayed! it had been good for that man if he had not been born.

15 Then Judas, which betrayed him, answered and said, [Judas] Master, is it I? He said unto him, [Jesus] Thou hast said.

MARK 14:18–21

18 And as they sat and did eat, Jesus said, [Jesus] Verily I say unto you, One of you which eateth with me shall betray me.

19 And they began to be sorrowful, and to say unto him one by one, [Disciples] Is it I? and another said, [Disciple] Is it I?

20 And he answered and said unto them, [Jesus] It is one of the twelve, that dippeth with me in the dish.

21 The Son of man indeed goeth, as it is written of him: but woe to that man by whom the Son of man is betrayed! good were it for that man if he had never been born.

LUKE 22:21–23

21 [Jesus] But, behold, the hand of him that betrayeth me is with me on the table.

22 And truly the Son of man goeth, as it was determined: but woe unto that man by whom he is betrayed.

23 And they began to inquire among themselves, which of them it was that should do this thing.

JOHN 13:18–30

18 [Jesus] I speak not of you all: I know whom I have chosen: but that the scripture may be fulfilled, He that eateth bread with me hath lifted up his heel against me.

19 Now I tell you before it come, that, when it is come to pass, ye may believe that I am he.

20 Verily, verily, I say unto you, He that receiveth whomsoever I send receiveth me; and he that receive me receiveth him that sent me.

21 When Jesus had thus said, he was troubled in spirit, and testified, and said, [**Jesus**] **Verily, verily, I say unto you, that one of you shall betray me.**

22 Then the disciples looked one on another, doubting of whom he spake.

23 Now there was leaning on Jesus' bosom one of his disciples, whom Jesus loved.

24 Simon Peter therefore beckoned to him, that he should ask who it should be of whom he spake.

25 He then lying on Jesus' breast saith unto him, [**John the Beloved**] **Lord, who is it?**

26 Jesus answered, [**Jesus**] **He it is, to whom I shall give a sop, when I have dipped it.** And when he had dipped the sop, he gave it to Judas Iscariot, the son of Simon.

27 And after the sop Satan entered into him. Then said Jesus unto him, [**Jesus**] **That thou doest, do quickly.**

28 Now no man at the table knew for what intent he spake this unto him.

29 For some of them thought, because Judas had the bag, that Jesus had said unto him, Buy those things that we have need of against the feast; or, that he should give something to the poor.

30 He then having received the sop went immediately out: and it was night.

42

A NEW COMMANDMENT

JOHN 13:33–35
Location: Jerusalem

Summary

After dismissing His betrayer, the Lord referred to His disciples as little children. We are as infants to the Lord given His majesty, intellect, and power, and yet He shows such tender love to all. Jesus told His disciples that they could not go where He was going. I suspect they had no clue what He was telling them. He was going to die and return to His Father. Then He gave them a new commandment that they love one another as He had loved them. He told them that this attribute is a trademark of discipleship . . . if ye have love one to another.

JOHN 13:33–35

33 [Jesus] Little children, yet a little while I am with you. Ye shall seek me: and as I said unto the Jews, Whither I go, ye cannot come; so now I say to you.

34 A new commandment I give unto you, That ye love one another; as I have loved you, that ye also love one another.

35 By this shall all men know that ye are my disciples, if ye have love one to another.

43

SACRAMENT INSTITUTED

MATTHEW 26:26–29; MARK 14:22–25;
LUKE 22:15–20
Location: Jerusalem

Summary

The Savior instituted the ordinance of the sacrament with His remaining Apostles. He first took bread (symbolic of His body) and broke it (symbolic of His broken flesh) and asked them to eat and do this in remembrance of Him. Next, He took wine and gives thanks (prayed) and told the Apostles that this was His blood (symbolic of His sacrifice), which would be shed for the remission of sins (the Atonement). Then He told them that He would not drink of the vine anymore until He drank it anew in the Kingdom of God.

The Savior taught them about His forthcoming sacrifice and what it would accomplish, and He provided a way for them to remember His sacrifice for all of God's children.

MATTHEW 26:26–29

26 And as they were eating, Jesus took bread, and blessed it, and brake it, and gave it to the disciples, and said, [**Jesus**] **Take, eat; this is my body.**

27 And he took the cup, and gave thanks, and gave it to them, saying, [**Jesus**] **Drink ye all of it;**

28 For this is my blood of the new testament, which is shed for many for the remission of sins.

29 But I say unto you, I will not drink henceforth of this fruit of the vine, until that day when I drink it new with you in my Father's kingdom.

JST, MATTHEW 26:22, 24–25.

Compare Matthew 26:26–28; JST, Mark 14:20–25.
Jesus first breaks the sacramental bread then blesses it. The sacrament is in remembrance of Jesus' body and blood.

22 And as they were eating, Jesus took bread and brake it, and blessed it, and gave to his disciples, and said, [Jesus] Take, eat; this is in remembrance of my body which I give a ransom for you.

24 For this is in remembrance of my blood of the new testament, which is shed for as many as shall believe on my name, for the remission of their sins.

25 And I give unto you a commandment, that ye shall observe to do the things which ye have seen me do, and bear record of me even unto the end.

MARK 14:22–25

22 And as they did eat, Jesus took bread, and blessed, and brake it, and gave to them, and said, [Jesus] Take, eat: this is my body.

23 And he took the cup, and when he had given thanks, he gave it to them: and they all drank of it.

24 And he said unto them, [Jesus] This is my blood of the new testament, which is shed for many.

25 Verily I say unto you, I will drink no more of the fruit of the vine, until that day that I drink it new in the kingdom of God.

JST, MARK 14:20–26.

Compare Mark 14:22–25.
Jesus institutes the sacrament in remembrance of His body and blood.

20 And as they did eat, Jesus took bread and blessed it, and brake, and gave to them, and said, [Jesus] Take it, and eat.

21 Behold, this is for you to do in remembrance of my body; for as oft as ye do this ye will remember this hour that I was with you.

22 And he took the cup, and when he had given thanks, he gave it to them; and they all drank of it.

23 And he said unto them, [Jesus] This is in remembrance of my blood which is shed for many, and the new testament which I give unto you; for of me ye shall bear record unto all the world.

24 And as oft as ye do this ordinance, ye will remember me in this hour that I was with you and drank with you of this cup, even the last time in my ministry.

25 Verily I say unto you, Of this ye shall bear record; for I will no more drink of the fruit of the vine with you, until that day that I drink it new in the kingdom of God.

26 And now they were grieved, and wept over him.

LUKE 22:15–20

15 And he said unto them, [Jesus] With desire I have desired to eat this passover with you before I suffer:

16 For I say unto you, I will not any more eat thereof, until it be fulfilled in the kingdom of God.

17 And he took the cup, and gave thanks, and said, [Jesus] Take this, and divide it among yourselves:

18 For I say unto you, I will not drink of the fruit of the vine, until the kingdom of God shall come.

19 And he took bread, and gave thanks, and brake it, and gave unto them, saying, [Jesus] This is my body which is given for you: this do in remembrance of me.

20 Likewise also the cup after supper, saying, This cup is the new testament in my blood, which is shed for you.

44

DISCOURSE ON
THE COMFORTER

JOHN 14
Location: Jerusalem

Summary

The Savior taught His disciples five fundamental gospel principles before He departed to the Mount of Olives:

1. In His Father's house are many mansions. He was going to prepare a place for them.
2. If they would follow Him, the Lord Jesus Christ, they would always know the way they should go.
3. Because they had seen Him, they had seen the Father. In other words, the Savior has the same characteristics and attributes as the Father has. They are completely in sync. Therefore, if the Apostles wanted to know about the Father, all they had to do was know the Savior.
4. The Holy Ghost, also known as the Comforter, would teach them all things and bring all things to their remembrance.
5. They shouldn't let their hearts be troubled nor be afraid because they could have the peace of the Lord.

JOHN 14

1 [Jesus] **Let not your heart be troubled: ye believe in God, believe also in me.**

2 In my Father's house are many mansions: if it were not so, I would have told you. I go to prepare a place for you.

3 And if I go and prepare a place for you, I will come again, and receive you unto myself; that where I am, there ye may be also.

4 And whither I go ye know, and the way ye know.

5 Thomas saith unto him, [Thomas] Lord, we know not whither thou goest; and how can we know the way?

6 Jesus saith unto him, [Jesus] I am the way, the truth, and the life: no man cometh unto the Father, but by me.

7 If ye had known me, ye should have known my Father also: and from henceforth ye know him, and have seen him.

8 Philip saith unto him, [Philip] Lord, shew us the Father, and it sufficeth us.

9 Jesus saith unto him, [Jesus] Have I been so long time with you, and yet hast thou not known me, Philip? he that hath seen me hath seen the Father; and how sayest thou then, Shew us the Father?

10 Believest thou not that I am in the Father, and the Father in me? the words that I speak unto you I speak not of myself: but the Father that dwelleth in me, he doeth the works.

11 Believe me that I am in the Father, and the Father in me: or else believe me for the very works' sake.

12 Verily, verily, I say unto you, He that believeth on me, the works that I do shall he do also; and greater works than these shall he do; because I go unto my Father.

13 And whatsoever ye shall ask in my name, that will I do, that the Father may be glorified in the Son.

14 If ye shall ask any thing in my name, I will do it.

15 If ye love me, keep my commandments.

16 And I will pray the Father, and he shall give you another Comforter, that he may abide with you for ever;

17 Even the Spirit of truth; whom the world cannot receive, because it seeth him not, neither knoweth him:

but ye know him; for he dwelleth with you, and shall be in you.

18 I will not leave you comfortless: I will come to you.

19 Yet a little while, and the world seeth me no more; but ye see me: because I live, ye shall live also.

20 At that day ye shall know that I am in my Father, and ye in me, and I in you.

21 He that hath my commandments, and keepeth them, he it is that loveth me: and he that loveth me shall be loved of my Father, and I will love him, and will manifest myself to him.

22 Judas saith unto him, not Iscariot, [Judas, not Iscariot] Lord, how is it that thou wilt manifest thyself unto us, and not unto the world?

23 Jesus answered and said unto him, [Jesus] If a man love me, he will keep my words: and my Father will love him, and we will come unto him, and make our abode with him.

24 He that loveth me not keepeth not my sayings: and the word which ye hear is not mine, but the Father's which sent me.

25 These things have I spoken unto you, being yet present with you.

26 But the Comforter, which is the Holy Ghost, whom the Father will send in my name, he shall teach you all things, and bring all things to your remembrance, whatsoever I have said unto you.

27 Peace I leave with you, my peace I give unto you: not as the world giveth, give I unto you. Let not your heart be troubled, neither let it be afraid.

28 Ye have heard how I said unto you, I go away, and come again unto you. If ye loved me, ye would rejoice, because I said, I go unto the Father: for my Father is greater than I.

29 And now I have told you before it come to pass, that, when it is come to pass, ye might believe.

30 Hereafter I will not talk much with you: for the prince of this world cometh, and hath nothing in me.

31 But that the world may know that I love the Father; and as the Father gave me commandment, even so I do. Arise, let us go hence.

JST, JOHN 14:30
Compare John 14:30.
The prince of darkness, or Satan, is of this world.

30 [Jesus] Hereafter I will not talk much with you; for the prince of darkness, who is of this world, cometh, but hath no power over me, but he hath power over you.

45

DEPARTURE TO MOUNT OF OLIVES

MATTHEW 26:30; MARK 14:26; LUKE 22:39;
JOHN 14:31
Location: Jerusalem

Summary

After singing a hymn, the Savior and His disciples departed for the Mount of Olives.

MATTHEW 26:30

30 And when they had sung an hymn, they went out into the mount of Olives.

MARK 14:26

26 And when they had sung an hymn, they went out into the mount of Olives.

LUKE 22:39

39 And he came out, and went, as he was wont, to the mount of Olives; and his disciples also followed him.

JOHN 14:31

31 [Jesus] But that the world may know that I love
the Father; and as the Father gave me commandment,
even so I do. Arise, let us go hence.

46

PETER'S DENIAL FORETOLD

MATTHEW 26:31–35; MARK 14:27–31;
LUKE 22:31–38; JOHN 13:36–38
Location: Jerusalem

Summary

The Savior prophesied to the disciples that before the night was over, they would distance themselves from Him. Peter was bold and said that he would never be offended by being with the Lord and that he would follow Him into prison or death before he would distance himself from the Lord. Then came the Lord's seminal prophecy: "The cock shall not crow, till thou hast denied me thrice" (John 13:38). Peter loved the Lord and wanted to support Him through all things, but in times of great difficulty, he was unable to persevere.

MATTHEW 26:31–35

31 Then saith Jesus unto them, **[Jesus] All ye shall be offended because of me this night: for it is written, I will smite the shepherd, and the sheep of the flock shall be scattered abroad.**

32 **But after I am risen again, I will go before you into Galilee.**

33 Peter answered and said unto him, **[Peter] Though all men shall be offended because of thee, yet will I never be offended.**

34 Jesus said unto him, [Jesus] Verily I say unto thee, That this night, before the cock crow, thou shalt deny me thrice.

35 Peter said unto him, [Peter] Though I should die with thee, yet will I not deny thee. Likewise also said all the disciples.

MARK 14:27–31

27 And Jesus saith unto them, [Jesus] All ye shall be offended because of me this night: for it is written, I will smite the shepherd, and the sheep shall be scattered.

28 But after that I am risen, I will go before you into Galilee.

29 But Peter said unto him, [Peter] Although all shall be offended, yet will not I.

30 And Jesus saith unto him, [Jesus] Verily I say unto thee, That this day, even in this night, before the cock crow twice, thou shalt deny me thrice.

31 But he spake the more vehemently, [Peter] If I should die with thee, I will not deny thee in any wise. Likewise also said they all.

LUKE 22:31–38

31 And the Lord said, [Jesus] Simon, Simon, behold, Satan hath desired to have you, that he may sift you as wheat:

32 But I have prayed for thee, that thy faith fail not: and when thou art converted, strengthen thy brethren.

33 And he said unto him, [Peter] Lord, I am ready to go with thee, both into prison, and to death.

34 And he said, [Jesus] I tell thee, Peter, the cock shall not crow this day, before that thou shalt thrice deny that thou knowest me.

35 And he said unto them, When I sent you without purse, and scrip, and shoes, lacked ye any thing? And they said, Nothing.

36 Then said he unto them, But now, he that hath a purse, let him take it, and likewise his scrip: and he that hath no sword, let him sell his garment, and buy one.

37 For I say unto you, that this that is written must yet be accomplished in me, And he was reckoned among the transgressors: for the things concerning me have an end.

38 And they said, [Disciples] Lord, behold, here are two swords. And he said unto them, It is enough.

JOHN 13:36–38

36 Simon Peter said unto him, [Peter] Lord, whither goest thou? Jesus answered him, [Jesus] Whither I go, thou canst not follow me now; but thou shalt follow me afterwards.

37 Peter said unto him, [Peter] Lord, why cannot I follow thee now? I will lay down my life for thy sake.

38 Jesus answered him, [Jesus] Wilt thou lay down thy life for my sake? Verily, verily, I say unto thee, The cock shall not crow, till thou hast denied me thrice.

47

THE TRUE VINE

JOHN 15:1–8
Location: Jerusalem

Summary

The Savior testified that He is the true vine. If we follow Him, we will bring forth much fruit. However, without Him we can do nothing.

JOHN 15:1–8

1 [Jesus] I am the true vine, and my Father is the husbandman.

2 Every branch in me that beareth not fruit he taketh away: and every branch that beareth fruit, he purgeth it, that it may bring forth more fruit.

3 Now ye are clean through the word which I have spoken unto you.

4 Abide in me, and I in you. As the branch cannot bear fruit of itself, except it abide in the vine; no more can ye, except ye abide in me.

5 I am the vine, ye are the branches: He that abideth in me, and I in him, the same bringeth forth much fruit: for without me ye can do nothing.

6 If a man abide not in me, he is cast forth as a branch, and is withered; and men gather them, and cast them into the fire, and they are burned.

7 If ye abide in me, and my words abide in you, ye shall ask what ye will, and it shall be done unto you.

8 Herein is my Father glorified, that ye bear much fruit; so shall ye be my disciples.

48

LOVE ONE ANOTHER

JOHN 15:9–17
Location: Jerusalem

Summary

The Savior taught the disciples about the importance of keeping His commandments, which includes loving one another. He told them that if they would keep His commandments and love one another, they would abide in His love. What a wonderful promise for each of us!

JOHN 15:9–17

9 [Jesus] As the Father hath loved me, so have I loved you: continue ye in my love.

10 If ye keep my commandments, ye shall abide in my love; even as I have kept my Father's commandments, and abide in his love.

11 These things have I spoken unto you, that my joy might remain in you, and that your joy might be full.

12 This is my commandment, That ye love one another, as I have loved you.

13 Greater love hath no man than this, that a man lay down his life for his friends.

14 Ye are my friends, if ye do whatsoever I command you.

15 Henceforth I call you not servants; for the servant knoweth not what his lord doeth: but I have called you

friends; for all things that I have heard of my Father I have made known unto you.

16 Ye have not chosen me, but I have chosen you, and ordained you, that ye should go and bring forth fruit, and that your fruit should remain: that whatsoever ye shall ask of the Father in my name, he may give it you.

17 These things I command you, that ye love one another.

49

HATRED OF THE WORLD

JOHN 15:18–25
Location: Jerusalem

Summary

The Lord taught the disciples the reason they were hated by men—they were not of the world. He pointed out that He was also hated by men and therefore His followers shouldn't expect anything different.

JOHN 15:18–25

18 [Jesus] If the world hate you, ye know that it hated me before it hated you.

19 If ye were of the world, the world would love his own: but because ye are not of the world, but I have chosen you out of the world, therefore the world hateth you.

20 Remember the word that I said unto you, The servant is not greater than his lord. If they have persecuted me, they will also persecute you; if they have kept my saying, they will keep yours also.

21 But all these things will they do unto you for my name's sake, because they know not him that sent me.

22 If I had not come and spoken unto them, they had not had sin: but now they have no cloak for their sin.

23 He that hateth me hateth my Father also.

24 If I had not done among them the works which none other man did, they had not had sin: but now have they both seen and hated both me and my Father.

25 But this cometh to pass, that the word might be fulfilled that is written in their law, They hated me without a cause.

50

THE SPIRIT OF
TRUTH TESTIFIES

JOHN 15:26–27
Location: Jerusalem

Summary

The Savior taught His disciples that He would send the Holy Ghost (the Comforter) to them from the Father. These scriptures are clear that the Holy Ghost is sent from the Father to teach truth and to testify of the Savior. Jesus also taught His disciples that they should bear witness of the divinity of the Savior because they were with Him from the beginning of His ministry and had firsthand experience with Him and His divine mission.

Besides testifying of the divinity of the Savior's mission, the Holy Ghost is also sent to provide comfort and testify of truth.

> **JOHN 15:26–27**
>
> 26 [Jesus] But when the Comforter is come, whom I will send unto you from the Father, even the Spirit of truth, which proceedeth from the Father, he shall testify of me:
>
> 27 And ye also shall bear witness, because ye have been with me from the beginning.

51

WARNINGS TO THE APOSTLES

JOHN 16:1–6
Location: Jerusalem

Summary

The Savior warned the Apostles that they would be persecuted and even killed because of their association with Him. I believe that He wanted them to remember this so when they experienced persecution their testimony would be strengthened and they would have increased ability to endure. These teachings were an act of love on the Lord's part so that the Apostles would be able to endure persecution and return to live with Him again. The same could be said of the revelations and teachings that we have before us today. All of it is preparation for us as we make it through this mortal sojourn.

> **JOHN 16:1–6**
>
> 1 [Jesus] These things have I spoken unto you, that ye should not be offended.
>
> 2 They shall put you out of the synagogues: yea, the time cometh, that whosoever killeth you will think that he doeth God service.
>
> 3 And these things will they do unto you, because they have not known the Father, nor me.

4 But these things have I told you, that when the time shall come, ye may remember that I told you of them. And these things I said not unto you at the beginning, because I was with you.

5 But now I go my way to him that sent me; and none of you asketh me, Whither goest thou?

6 But because I have said these things unto you, sorrow hath filled your heart.

52

THE COMFORTER

JOHN 16:7–16
Location: Jerusalem

Summary

The Savior taught the Apostles about the Comforter. He first said that while He, the Lord, was with them, the Comforter wouldn't be. He then said that the Comforter is the Spirit of truth (a revelator) and would come to guide them and show them things to come. The Holy Ghost would also come to glorify Him. Last, the Lord taught that He would soon go to the Father and would no longer be with them, suggesting that the Comforter would be sent in His stead.

> **JOHN 16:7–16**
>
> 7 [Jesus] Nevertheless I tell you the truth; It is expedient for you that I go away: for if I go not away, the Comforter will not come unto you; but if I depart, I will send him unto you.
>
> 8 And when he is come, he will reprove the world of sin, and of righteousness, and of judgment:
>
> 9 Of sin, because they believe not on me;
>
> 10 Of righteousness, because I go to my Father, and ye see me no more;

11 Of judgment, because the prince of this world is judged.

12 I have yet many things to say unto you, but ye cannot bear them now.

13 Howbeit when he, the Spirit of truth, is come, he will guide you into all truth: for he shall not speak of himself; but whatsoever he shall hear, that shall he speak: and he will shew you things to come.

14 He shall glorify me: for he shall receive of mine, and shall shew it unto you.

15 All things that the Father hath are mine: therefore said I, that he shall take of mine, and shall shew it unto you.

16 A little while, and ye shall not see me: and again, a little while, and ye shall see me, because I go to the Father.

53

OPPOSITION: JOY AND SORROW

JOHN 16:17–30

Location: Jerusalem

Summary

The Savior began to teach about His death and resurrection by explaining to the Apostles that they would feel sorrow and weep and lament. But afterward, they would feel great joy. The period of mourning would occur when He died on the cross, but great joy would come when they saw Him resurrected. He compared this to a mother who delivers a child. She feels sadness and experiences great pain during childbirth, but immediately feels great joy when she sees the child. After teaching this principle, the Lord taught that after His death the Apostles were to pray to the Father in His name.

> **JOHN 16:17–30**
>
> 17 Then said some of his disciples among themselves, **[Disciples] What is this that he saith unto us, A little while, and ye shall not see me: and again, a little while, and ye shall see me: and, Because I go to the Father?**
>
> 18 They said therefore, **[Disciples] What is this that he saith, A little while? we cannot tell what he saith.**

19 Now Jesus knew that they were desirous to ask him, and said unto them, [Jesus] Do ye inquire among yourselves of that I said, A little while, and ye shall not see me: and again, a little while, and ye shall see me?

20 Verily, verily, I say unto you, That ye shall weep and lament, but the world shall rejoice: and ye shall be sorrowful, but your sorrow shall be turned into joy.

21 A woman when she is in travail hath sorrow, because her hour is come: but as soon as she is delivered of the child, she remembereth no more the anguish, for joy that a man is born into the world.

22 And ye now therefore have sorrow: but I will see you again, and your heart shall rejoice, and your joy no man taketh from you.

23 And in that day ye shall ask me nothing. Verily, verily, I say unto you, Whatsoever ye shall ask the Father in my name, he will give it you.

24 Hitherto have ye asked nothing in my name: ask, and ye shall receive, that your joy may be full.

25 These things have I spoken unto you in proverbs: but the time cometh, when I shall no more speak unto you in proverbs, but I shall shew you plainly of the Father.

26 At that day ye shall ask in my name: and I say not unto you, that I will pray the Father for you:

27 For the Father himself loveth you, because ye have loved me, and have believed that I came out from God.

28 I came forth from the Father, and am come into the world: again, I leave the world, and go to the Father.

29 His disciples said unto him, [Disciples] Lo, now speakest thou plainly, and speakest no proverb.

30 Now are we sure that thou knowest all things, and needest not that any man should ask thee: by this we believe that thou camest forth from God.

54

JESUS' INTERCESSORY PRAYER

JOHN 17
Location: Jerusalem

Summary

As the Lord began His intercessory prayer, He pointed out that the hour had come. He asked the Father to glorify Him that He may glorify the Father. The Lord then offered the seminal statement: "And this is life eternal, that they might know thee the only true God, and Jesus Christ, whom thou hast sent" (John 17:3). Although part of the prayer, He taught the Apostles how they might obtain eternal life—they must come to know the Father and the Son.

Next, the Lord asked the Father to glorify Him with the glory that He had before the world was, which taught the Apostles about the Lord's premortal existence. The Lord also prayed for His beloved Apostles by asking that they may be united as He is united with the Father. He also asked that His followers may be sanctified and united with Him. He concluded His prayer by asking the Father to love His followers as the Father has loved His beloved Son. What a wonderful intercessory prayer that the Lord makes before going to Gethsemane.

JOHN 17

1 These words spake Jesus, and lifted up his eyes to heaven, and said, [Jesus] Father, the hour is come; glorify thy Son, that thy Son also may glorify thee:

2 As thou hast given him power over all flesh, that he should give eternal life to as many as thou hast given him.

3 And this is life eternal, that they might know thee the only true God, and Jesus Christ, whom thou hast sent.

4 I have glorified thee on the earth: I have finished the work which thou gavest me to do.

5 And now, O Father, glorify thou me with thine own self with the glory which I had with thee before the world was.

6 I have manifested thy name unto the men which thou gavest me out of the world: thine they were, and thou gavest them me; and they have kept thy word.

7 Now they have known that all things whatsoever thou hast given me are of thee.

8 For I have given unto them the words which thou gavest me; and they have received them, and have known surely that I came out from thee, and they have believed that thou didst send me.

9 I pray for them: I pray not for the world, but for them which thou hast given me; for they are thine.

10 And all mine are thine, and thine are mine; and I am glorified in them.

11 And now I am no more in the world, but these are in the world, and I come to thee. Holy Father, keep through thine own name those whom thou hast given me, that they may be one, as we are.

12 While I was with them in the world, I kept them in thy name: those that thou gavest me I have kept, and none of them is lost, but the son of perdition; that the scripture might be fulfilled.

13 And now come I to thee; and these things I speak in the world, that they might have my joy fulfilled in themselves.

14 I have given them thy word; and the world hath hated them, because they are not of the world, even as I am not of the world.

15 I pray not that thou shouldest take them out of the world, but that thou shouldest keep them from the evil.

16 They are not of the world, even as I am not of the world.

17 Sanctify them through thy truth: thy word is truth.

18 As thou hast sent me into the world, even so have I also sent them into the world.

19 And for their sakes I sanctify myself, that they also might be sanctified through the truth.

20 Neither pray I for these alone, but for them also which shall believe on me through their word;

21 That they all may be one; as thou, Father, art in me, and I in thee, that they also may be one in us: that the world may believe that thou hast sent me.

22 And the glory which thou gavest me I have given them; that they may be one, even as we are one:

23 I in them, and thou in me, that they may be made perfect in one; and that the world may know that thou hast sent me, and hast loved them, as thou hast loved me.

24 Father, I will that they also, whom thou hast given me, be with me where I am; that they may behold my glory, which thou hast given me: for thou lovedst me before the foundation of the world.

25 O righteous Father, the world hath not known thee: but I have known thee, and these have known that thou hast sent me.

26 And I have declared unto them thy name, and will declare it: that the love wherewith thou hast loved me may be in them, and I in them.

55

JESUS' SUFFERING AND PRAYERS

MATTHEW 26:36–46; MARK 14:32–42;
LUKE 22: 40–46; JOHN 18:1
Location: Gethsemane

Summary

The Savior walked to Gethsemane with His Apostles, and He told eight of them to wait while He went a little farther with Peter, James, and John. He began to be sorrowful and very heavy, and He told His Apostles, "My soul is exceeding sorrowful, even unto death" (Matthew 26:38). He instructed them to wait and watch with Him, and then He went a little farther (about a stone's cast), where He "prayed, saying, O my Father, if it be possible, let this cup pass from me: nevertheless not as I will, but as thou wilt" (Matthew 26:42). The burden was intense, and He asked the Father to intervene if there was another way. But if not, He would do the will of the Father. This request suggests that even the Lord Himself may not have fully understood the intense suffering that the Atonement would bring.

The Savior must have been praying for about an hour because He returned to the three Apostles and found them asleep. He asked Peter, "What, could ye not watch with me one hour? Watch and pray, that ye enter not into temptation: the spirit indeed is willing, but the flesh is weak" (Matthew 26:40–41).

Then the Savior went away again and pleaded with His Father, saying "O my Father, if this cup may not pass away from me, except I drink it, thy will be done" (Matthew 26:42–44). Afterward, he returned to His brethren and found them asleep again, so he went away a third time and prayed to His Father the same words. This is when an angel appeared to strengthen Him. The Gospel account then reveals that "His sweat was as it were great drops of blood falling down to the ground" (Luke 22:44–46). After fulfilling this aspect of the Atonement, the Savior returned to His brethren, who were sleeping, and He invited them to "rise, let us be going: behold, he is at hand that doth betray me" (Luke 22:44–46).

Related Scriptures and Thoughts

DOCTRINE AND COVENANTS 18:11

For, behold the Lord Your Redeemer suffered death in the flesh; wherefore he suffered the pain of all men, that all men might repent and come unto him."

ISAIAH 53:3–4

He is despised and rejected of men; a man of sorrows, and acquainted with grief: and we hid as it were our faces from him; he was despised, and we esteemed him not. Surely he hath borne our griefs, and carried our sorrows: yet we did esteem him stricken, smitten of God, and afflicted.

MOSIAH 3:7

And lo, he shall suffer temptations, and pain of body, hunger, thirst, and fatigue, even more than man can suffer, except it be unto death; for behold, blood cometh from every pore, so great shall be his anguish for the wickedness and the abominations of his people.

JAMES E. TALMAGE, JESUS THE CHRIST

Christ's agony in the garden is unfathomable by the finite mind, both as to intensity and cause. . . . He struggled and groaned under a burden such as no other being who has lived on earth might even conceive as possible. It was not physical pain, nor mental anguish alone, that

135

caused him to suffer such torture as to produce an extrusion of blood from every pore; but a spiritual agony of soul such as only God was capable of experiencing. No other man, however great his powers of physical or mental endurance, could have suffered so; for his human organism would have succumbed, and syncope would have produced unconsciousness and welcome oblivion. . . .

In some manner, actual and terribly real though to man incomprehensible, the Savior took upon himself the burden of the sins of mankind from Adam to the end of the world. Modern revelation assists us to a partial understanding of the awful experience. In March 1830, the glorified Lord, Jesus Christ, thus spake: "For behold, I, God, have suffered these things for all, that they might not suffer if they would repent, but if they would not repent, then must suffer even as I, which suffering caused myself, even God, the greatest of all, to tremble because of pain, and to bleed at every port, and to suffer both body and spirit: and would that I might not drink the bitter cup and shrink—nevertheless, glory be to the Father, and I partook and finished my preparations unto the children of men."

From the terrible conflict in Gethsemane, Christ emerged a victor. Though in the dark tribulation of the fearful hour he had pleaded that the bitter cup be removed from his lips, the request, however oft repeated, was always conditional; the accomplishment of the Father's will was never lost sight of as the object of the Son's supreme desire. The further tragedy of the night, and the cruel inflictions that awaited him on the marrow, to culminate in the frightful tortures of the cross, could not exceed the bitter anguish through which he had successfully passed.[38]

—·—

MATTHEW 26:36–46

36 Then cometh Jesus with them unto a place called Gethsemane, and saith unto the disciples, [**Disciples**] **Sit ye here, while I go and pray yonder.**

37 And he took with him Peter and the two sons of Zebedee, and began to be sorrowful and very heavy.

38 Then saith he unto them, [Jesus] **My soul is exceeding sorrowful, even unto death: tarry ye here, and watch with me.**

39 And he went a little further, and fell on his face, and prayed, saying, [Jesus] **O my Father, if it be possible, let this cup pass from me: nevertheless not as I will, but as thou wilt.**

40 And he cometh unto the disciples, and findeth them asleep, and saith unto Peter, [Jesus] **What, could ye not watch with me one hour?**

41 **Watch and pray, that ye enter not into temptation: the spirit indeed is willing, but the flesh is weak.**

42 He went away again the second time, and prayed, saying, [Jesus] **O my Father, if this cup may not pass away from me, except I drink it, thy will be done.**

43 And he came and found them asleep again: for their eyes were heavy.

44 And he left them, and went away again, and prayed the third time, saying the same words.

45 Then cometh he to his disciples, and saith unto them, [Jesus] **Sleep on now, and take your rest: behold, the hour is at hand, and the Son of man is betrayed into the hands of sinners.**

46 **Rise, let us be going: behold, he is at hand that doth betray me.**

MARK 14:32–42

32 And they came to a place which was named Gethsemane: and he saith to his disciples, [Jesus] **Sit ye here, while I shall pray.**

33 And he taketh with him Peter and James and John, and began to be sore amazed, and to be very heavy;

34 And saith unto them, [Jesus] **My soul is exceeding sorrowful unto death: tarry ye here, and watch.**

35 And he went forward a little, and fell on the ground, and prayed that, if it were possible, the hour might pass from him.

36 And he said, [Jesus] **Abba, Father, all things are possible unto thee; take away this cup from me: nevertheless not what I will, but what thou wilt.**

37 And he cometh, and findeth them sleeping, and saith unto Peter, Simon, [Jesus] **sleepest thou? couldest not thou watch one hour?**

38 Watch ye and pray, lest ye enter into temptation. The spirit truly is ready, but the flesh is weak.

39 And again he went away, and prayed, and spake the same words.

40 And when he returned, he found them asleep again, (for their eyes were heavy,) neither wist they what to answer him.

41 And he cometh the third time, and saith unto them, [Jesus] Sleep on now, and take your rest: it is enough, the hour is come; behold, the Son of man is betrayed into the hands of sinners.

42 Rise up, let us go; lo, he that betrayeth me is at hand.

JST, MARK 14:36–38

Compare Mark 14:32–34.

At Gethsemane, even the Twelve do not fully grasp Jesus' role as the Messiah.

36 And they came to a place which was named Gethsemane, which was a garden; and the disciples began to be sore amazed, and to be very heavy, and to complain in their hearts, wondering if this be the Messiah.

37 And Jesus knowing their hearts, said to his disciples, [Jesus] **Sit ye here, while I shall pray.**

38 And he taketh with him, Peter, and James, and John, and rebuked them, and said unto them, [Jesus] **My soul is exceeding sorrowful, even unto death; tarry ye here and watch.**

LUKE 22: 40–46

40 And when he was at the place, he said unto them, [Jesus] **Pray that ye enter not into temptation.**

41 And he was withdrawn from them about a stone's cast, and kneeled down, and prayed,

42 Saying, [Jesus] **Father, if thou be willing, remove this cup from me: nevertheless not my will, but thine, be done.**

43 And there appeared an angel unto him from heaven, strengthening him.

44 And being in an agony he prayed more earnestly: and his sweat was as it were great drops of blood falling down to the ground.

45 And when he rose up from prayer, and was come to his disciples, he found them sleeping for sorrow,

46 And said unto them, [Jesus] **Why sleep ye? rise and pray, lest ye enter into temptation.**

JOHN 18:1

1 When Jesus had spoken these words, he went forth with his disciples over the brook Cedron, where was a garden, into the which he entered, and his disciples.

56

JUDAS'S BETRAYAL

MATTHEW 26:47–50; MARK 14:43–46;
LUKE 22: 47–48; JOHN 18:2–3
Location: Gethsemane

Summary

After arising and greeting His disciples while still in the Garden of Geth-semane, the Savior and His Apostles were met by Judas and a "great multi-tude with swords and staves" (Matthew 26:47). The group was comprised of chief priests, scribes, and elders. Judas, who knew that this was a place where the Lord would often resort, had told those in the group that he would identify Jesus with a kiss and then they were to take Him. Judas stepped forward to greet the Lord with a kiss, and the Lord said unto him, "Judas, betrayest thou the Son of Man with a kiss?" (Luke 22:48).

Why did Judas have to identify the Lord with a kiss? It seems that the Savior had been among the residents of Jerusalem and among those who hated Him, and so they would have known Him well enough to identify Him without Judas's kiss. However, it is also reasonable that in order for the mob to bring Jesus up on charges that they would need a close associate, in this case Judas, to clearly identify Him as the person. This is often done in a courtroom, where a witness points out the perpetrator for the record even though all in attendance knows the person who is the accused.

MATTHEW 26:47–50

47 And while he yet spake, lo, Judas, one of the twelve, came, and with him a great multitude with swords and staves, from the chief priests and elders of the people.

48 Now he that betrayed him gave them a sign, saying, [Judas] **Whomsoever I shall kiss, that same is he: hold him fast.**

49 And forthwith he came to Jesus, and said, [Judas] **Hail, master; and kissed him.**

50 And Jesus said unto him, [Jesus] **Friend, wherefore art thou come?** Then came they, and laid hands on Jesus, and took him.

MARK 14:43–46

43 And immediately, while he yet spake, cometh Judas, one of the twelve, and with him a great multitude with swords and staves, from the chief priests and the scribes and the elders.

44 And he that betrayed him had given them a token, saying, [Judas] **Whomsoever I shall kiss, that same is he; take him, and lead him away safely.**

45 And as soon as he was come, he goeth straightway to him, and saith, [Judas] **Master, master; and kissed him.**

46 And they laid their hands on him, and took him.

LUKE 22: 47–48

47 And while he yet spake, behold a multitude, and he that was called Judas, one of the twelve, went before them, and drew near unto Jesus to kiss him.

48 But Jesus said unto him, [Jesus] **Judas, betrayest thou the Son of man with a kiss?**

JOHN 18:2–3

2 And Judas also, which betrayed him, knew the place: for Jesus oft times resorted thither with his disciples.

3 Judas then, having received a band of men and officers from the chief priests and Pharisees, cometh thither with lanterns and torches and weapons.

57

ARRESTING OFFICERS FALL

JOHN 18:4–9
Location: Gethsemane

Summary

It appears that when the Savior admitted to being Jesus of Nazareth, the people who asked stepped back and fell to the ground. Why it is not clear, perhaps, is that they were astonished by his majesty and purity. In other words, they may have wondered why they were seeking this holy man. In any regard, the Savior then stepped forward and asked that His disciples, who were with him, be released. "Let these go their way," (John 18:8) the Lord said, suggesting that He wanted to protect His beloved brethren.

JOHN 18:4–9

4 Jesus therefore, knowing all things that should come upon him, went forth, and said unto them, [**Jesus**] **Whom seek ye?**

5 They answered him, [**Mob**] **Jesus of Nazareth.** Jesus saith unto them, [**Jesus**] **I am he.** And Judas also, which betrayed him, stood with them.

6 As soon then as he had said unto them, I am he, they went backward, and fell to the ground.

7 Then asked he them again, [Jesus] **Whom seek ye?** And they said, [Mob] **Jesus of Nazareth.**

8 Jesus answered, [Jesus] **I have told you that I am he: if therefore ye seek me, let these go their way:**

9 That the saying might be fulfilled, which he spake, Of them which thou gavest me have I lost none.

58

PETER DEFENDS JESUS WITH A SWORD

MATTHEW 26:51–55; MARK 14:47;
LUKE 22:49–51; JOHN 18:10–11
Location: Gethsemane

Summary

After being met by the mob, Peter, in his enthusiasm to protect the Lord, drew his sword and smote off the ear of Malchus, one of the servants of the high priest. The Lord immediately reproved Peter and told him that this approach was not His way and reminded Peter that He could call down twelve legions of angels if He desired. The Lord also reminded him that He was fulfilling the will of the Father and was going to see this through. The Lord then restored the servant's ear and healed him.

This profound event provides several important teachings. First and foremost, the Lord was fulfilling the will of the Father and was committed to doing so. Second, the Lord was doing this of His own free will. He could have stopped it at any time, but He didn't. Third, He had power over all things, including the ability to restore the ear of the servant. Incredibly, the people who witnessed this event didn't immediately fall and worship the Lord. It is a testimony of the hard-heartedness that some people develop; even in the face of great miracles they will not believe.

MATTHEW 26:51–55

51 And, behold, one of them which were with Jesus stretched out his hand, and drew his sword, and struck a servant of the high priest's, and smote off his ear.

52 Then said Jesus unto him, [Jesus] **Put up again thy sword into his place: for all they that take the sword shall perish with the sword.**

53 **Thinkest thou that I cannot now pray to my Father, and he shall presently give me more than twelve legions of angels?**

54 **But how then shall the scriptures be fulfilled, that thus it must be?**

55 In that same hour said Jesus to the multitudes, [Jesus] **Are ye come out as against a thief with swords and staves for to take me? I sat daily with you teaching in the temple, and ye laid no hold on me.**

MARK 14:47

47 And one of them that stood by drew a sword, and smote a servant of the high priest, and cut off his ear.

LUKE 22:49–51

49 When they which were about him saw what would follow, they said unto him, [Disciples] **Lord, shall we smite with the sword?**

50 And one of them smote the servant of the high priest, and cut off his right ear.

51 And Jesus answered and said, [Jesus] **Suffer ye thus far.** And he touched his ear, and healed him.

JOHN 18:10–11

10 Then Simon Peter having a sword drew it, and smote the high priest's servant, and cut off his right ear. The servant's name was Malchus.

11 Then said Jesus unto Peter, [Jesus] **Put up thy sword into the sheath: the cup which my Father hath given me, shall I not drink it?**

59

JESUS ARRESTED AND DISCIPLES FLEE

MATTHEW 26:56–57; MARK 14:46–52;
LUKE 22:52–54; JOHN 18:12
Location: Gethsemane

Summary

After the initial encounter with the mob wherein Peter cut off the soldier's ear, the mob laid hold on Jesus to take him away to Caiaphas, the high priest, and to the place where the scribes and elders were assembled. Jesus pointed out to the chief priests that He was the same person that was in the temple with them daily. In other words, why were they approaching and dealing with Him in such an aggressive manner when He was one who taught daily in the temple, speaking to the point that the hearts of the people were hardened?

Mark points out that there was "a certain young man, having a linen cloth cast about his naked body" (Mark 14:51). This young man gave this cloth to the Savior and "fled from them naked" (verse 52). The mob then took the Lord to the high priest's house, and Peter followed "afar off," or in the distance (Luke 22:54).

MATTHEW 26:56–57

56 But all this was done, that the scriptures of the prophets might be fulfilled. Then all the disciples forsook him, and fled.

57 And they that had laid hold on Jesus led him away to Caiaphas the high priest, where the scribes and the elders were assembled.

MARK 14:46–52

46 And they laid their hands on him, and took him.

47 And one of them that stood by drew a sword, and smote a servant of the high priest, and cut off his ear.

48 And Jesus answered and said unto them, [Jesus] **Are ye come out, as against a thief, with swords and with staves to take me?**

49 **I was daily with you in the temple teaching, and ye took me not: but the scriptures must be fulfilled.**

50 And they all forsook him, and fled.

51 And there followed him a certain young man, having a linen cloth cast about his naked body; and the young men laid hold on him:

52 And he left the linen cloth, and fled from them naked.

LUKE 22:52–54

52 Then Jesus said unto the chief priests, and captains of the temple, and the elders, which were come to him, [Jesus] **Be ye come out, as against a thief, with swords and staves?**

53 **When I was daily with you in the temple, ye stretched forth no hands against me: but this is your hour, and the power of darkness.**

54 Then took they him, and led him, and brought him into the high priest's house. And Peter followed afar off.

JOHN 18:12

12 Then the band and the captain and officers of the Jews took Jesus, and bound him.

60

HEARING BEFORE CHIEF PRIESTS

MATTHEW 26:57–68; MARK 14:53–65;
LUKE 22:54; JOHN 18:13–16, 19–24
Location: Caiaphas's palace

Summary

After the mob laid their hands on the Savior, they led Him away first to Annas, the father-in-law of Caiaphas, the high priest, and then to the palace of Caiaphas, where the chief priests, scribes, and elders were assembled. Peter followed in the distance and then gathered with the servants of Caiaphas and warmed himself near the fire.

Once at the palace, all the council members sought false witnesses against the Lord so they could put Him to death. Some witnesses came forward, but their stories did not hold up. However, there were two who said, "This fellow said, I am able to destroy the temple of God, and build it in three days" (Matthew 26:61). With this, the high priest arose and demanded that Jesus address this accusation, but the Lord held His peace. Then the high priest said with greater intensity, "I adjure thee by the living god, that thou tell us whether thou be the Christ, the Son of God. Jesus saith unto him, Thou hast said: nevertheless I say unto you, Hereafter shall ye see the Son of man sitting on the right hand of power, and coming in the clouds of heaven" (verses 63–64).

This response sent the high priest into a frenzy wherein he rent his clothes and accused the Savior of blasphemy. The high priest then turned to the council and asked, "What think ye? They answered and said, He is guilty of death" (verse 66). They spit in the Lord's face, mocked Him, and smote Him with their palms.

MATTHEW 26:57–68

57 And they that had laid hold on Jesus led him away to Caiaphas the high priest, where the scribes and the elders were assembled.

58 But Peter followed him afar off unto the high priest's palace, and went in, and sat with the servants, to see the end.

59 Now the chief priests, and elders, and all the council, sought false witness against Jesus, to put him to death;

60 But found none: yea, though many false witnesses came, yet found they none. At the last came two false witnesses,

61 And said, [Two False Witnesses] **This fellow said, I am able to destroy the temple of God, and to build it in three days.**

62 And the high priest arose, and said unto him, [High Priest] **Answerest thou nothing? what is it which these witness against thee?**

63 But Jesus held his peace. And the high priest answered and said unto him, [High Priest] **I adjure thee by the living God, that thou tell us whether thou be the Christ, the Son of God.**

64 Jesus saith unto him, [Jesus] **Thou hast said: nevertheless I say unto you, Hereafter shall ye see the Son of man sitting on the right hand of power, and coming in the clouds of heaven.**

65 Then the high priest rent his clothes, saying, [High Priest] **He hath spoken blasphemy; what further need have we of witnesses? behold, now ye have heard his blasphemy.**

66 **What think ye?** They answered and said, [Mob] **He is guilty of death.**

67 Then did they spit in his face, and buffeted him; and others smote him with the palms of their hands,

68 Saying, **[Mob] Prophesy unto us, thou Christ, Who is he that smote thee?**

MARK 14:53–65

53 And they led Jesus away to the high priest: and with him were assembled all the chief priests and the elders and the scribes.

54 And Peter followed him afar off, even into the palace of the high priest: and he sat with the servants, and warmed himself at the fire.

55 And the chief priests and all the council sought for witness against Jesus to put him to death; and found none.

56 For many bare false witness against him, but their witness agreed not together.

57 And there arose certain, and bare false witness against him, saying,

58 We heard him say, I will destroy this temple that is made with hands, and within three days I will build another made without hands.

59 But neither so did their witness agree together.

60 And the high priest stood up in the midst, and asked Jesus, saying, **[High Priest] Answerest thou nothing? what is it which these witness against thee?**

61 But he held his peace, and answered nothing. Again the high priest asked him, and said unto him, **[High Priest] Art thou the Christ, the Son of the Blessed?**

62 And Jesus said, **[Jesus] I am: and ye shall see the Son of man sitting on the right hand of power, and coming in the clouds of heaven.**

63 Then the high priest rent his clothes, and saith, **[High Priest] What need we any further witnesses?**

64 **Ye have heard the blasphemy: what think ye?** And they all condemned him to be guilty of death.

65 And some began to spit on him, and to cover his face, and to buffet him, and to say unto him, **[Mob] Prophesy:** and the servants did strike him with the palms of their hands.

LUKE 22:54

54 Then took they him, and led him, and brought him into the high priest's house. And Peter followed afar off.

JOHN 18:13–16, 19–24

13 And led him away to Annas first; for he was father in law to Caiaphas, which was the high priest that same year.

14 Now Caiaphas was he, which gave counsel to the Jews, that it was expedient that one man should die for the people.

15 And Simon Peter followed Jesus, and so did another disciple: that disciple was known unto the high priest, and went in with Jesus into the palace of the high priest.

16 But Peter stood at the door without. Then went out that other disciple, which was known unto the high priest, and spake unto her that kept the door, and brought in Peter.

19 The high priest then asked Jesus of his disciples, and of his doctrine.

20 Jesus answered him, [Jesus] **I spake openly to the world; I ever taught in the synagogue, and in the temple, whither the Jews always resort; and in secret have I said nothing.**

21 **Why askest thou me? ask them which heard me, what I have said unto them: behold, they know what I said.**

22 And when he had thus spoken, one of the officers which stood by struck Jesus with the palm of his hand, saying, [Mob] **Answerest thou the high priest so?**

23 Jesus answered him, [Jesus] **If I have spoken evil, bear witness of the evil: but if well, why smitest thou me?**

24 Now Annas had sent him bound unto Caiaphas the high priest.

61

PETER'S DENIAL

MATTHEW 26:69–75; MARK 14:66–72;
LUKE 22:55–62; JOHN 18:17–18, 25–27
Location: Caiaphas's palace

Summary

As noted previously, Peter followed the mob in the distance until they came to the palace of Caiaphas, where Peter gathered around a fire to warm himself and to observe the proceedings of the council. No doubt Peter loved the Lord and wanted to know what was happening to Him. However, Peter was a mortal man who was naturally concerned with his own well-being. Previously, Jesus had told Peter that he would deny Him three times before the cock crowed thrice, but of course Peter argued that he would never deny the Lord. When this happened and Peter realized what he had done, he went out and wept bitterly. Of course, we know that later Peter became a powerful Apostle and ultimately gave his life for the Lord, but at this time he was still weak.

Does this experience resonate with us? We often express such devotion and strength in testimony, but when we encounter a challenge or difficulty, we succumb to the weakness of mortal man.

MATTHEW 26:69–75

69 Now Peter sat without in the palace: and a damsel-came unto him, saying, **[Damsel] Thou also wast with Jesus of Galilee.**

152

70 But he denied before them all, saying, [Peter] I know not what thou sayest.

71 And when he was gone out into the porch, another maid saw him, and said unto them that were there, [Another Maid] This fellow was also with Jesus of Nazareth.

72 And again he denied with an oath, [Peter] I do not know the man.

73 And after a while came unto him they that stood by, and said to Peter, [They that stood by] Surely thou also art one of them; for thy speech betrayeth thee.

74 Then began he to curse and to swear, saying, [Peter] I know not the man. And immediately the cock crew.

75 And Peter remembered the word of Jesus, which said unto him, Before the cock crow, thou shalt deny me thrice. And he went out, and wept bitterly.

MARK 14:66–72

66 And as Peter was beneath in the palace, there cometh one of the maids of the high priest:

67 And when she saw Peter warming himself, she looked upon him, and said, [Maid] And thou also wast with Jesus of Nazareth.

68 But he denied, saying, [Peter] I know not, neither understand I what thou sayest. And he went out into the porch; and the cock crew.

69 And a maid saw him again, and began to say to them that stood by, [Maid] This is one of them.

70 And he denied it again. And a little after, they that stood by said again to Peter, [They that stood by] Surely thou art one of them: for thou art a Galilæan, and thy speech agreeth thereto.

71 But he began to curse and to swear, saying, [Peter] I know not this man of whom ye speak.

72 And the second time the cock crew. And Peter called to mind the word that Jesus said unto him, Before the cock crow twice, thou shalt deny me thrice. And when he thought thereon, he wept.

LUKE 22:55–62

55 And when they had kindled a fire in the midst of the hall, and were set down together, Peter sat down among them.

56 But a certain maid beheld him as he sat by the fire, and earnestly looked upon him, and said, [**Maid**] **This man was also with him.**

57 And he denied him, saying, [**Peter**] **Woman, I know him not.**

58 And after a little while another saw him, and said, [**Another**] **Thou art also of them.** And Peter said, [**Peter**] **Man, I am not.**

59 And about the space of one hour after another confidently affirmed, saying, [**Another**] **Of a truth this fellow also was with him: for he is a Galilæan.**

60 And Peter said, [**Peter**] **Man, I know not what thou sayest.** And immediately, while he yet spake, the cock crew.

61 And the Lord turned, and looked upon Peter. And Peter remembered the word of the Lord, how he had said unto him, Before the cock crow, thou shalt deny me thrice.

62 And Peter went out, and wept bitterly.

JOHN 18:17–18, 25–27

17 Then saith the damsel that kept the door unto Peter, [**Damsel**] **Art not thou also one of this man's disciples?** He saith, [**Peter**] **I am not.**

18 And the servants and officers stood there, who had made a fire of coals; for it was cold: and they warmed themselves: and Peter stood with them, and warmed himself.

25 And Simon Peter stood and warmed himself. They said therefore unto him, [**Servants and Officers**] **Art not thou also one of his disciples?** He denied it, and said, [**Peter**] **I am not.**

26 One of the servants of the high priest, being his kinsman whose ear Peter cut off, saith, [**Servant of the High Priest**] **Did not I see thee in the garden with him?**

27 Peter then denied again: and immediately the cock crew.

62

SOLDIERS MOCK JESUS

LUKE 22:63–65
Location: Caiaphas's palace

Summary

The soldiers mocked Jesus and smote Him. Then they blindfolded Him and smote Him on the face. This physical torture in a blindfolded state would be horrific, because Jesus would not have known when the blow was coming. Then, after hitting Him in the face, they mocked Him by saying, "Now prophesy who hit you."

LUKE 22:63–65

63 And the men that held Jesus mocked him, and smote him.

64 And when they had blindfolded him, they struck him on the face, and asked him, saying, [**Soldiers**] **Prophesy, who is it that smote thee?**

65 And many other things blasphemously spake they against him.

63

HEARING BEFORE CAIAPHAS

MATTHEW 27:1; MARK 15:1; LUKE 22:66–71;
JOHN 18:24, 28
Location: Jerusalem

Summary

Early in the morning after an excruciating night of suffering in Gethsemane, the Lord was sent bound to Caiaphas, the high priest. While there, all the chief priests, elders, and scribes counseled together on how they might justify putting Jesus to death. It appears that they decided that the best approach would be to have Jesus commit blasphemy, which was a capital offense in their tradition. They reasoned that if they could get the Lord to claim He was the Christ that this would satisfy the requirement, so they asked Him directly, "Art thou the Christ?" Jesus said that it wouldn't matter how He responded because they had made up their mind and it wouldn't make any difference. He also told them that shortly He would sit on the right hand of God. Then they said, "Art thou then the Son of God?" The Lord responded, "Ye say that I am," and then they said, "What need we any further witness?" (See Luke 22:70–71.) With this response the council believed that Jesus had crossed the line and had committed blasphemy justifying death.

MATTHEW 27:1

1 When the morning was come, all the chief priests and elders of the people took counsel against Jesus to put him to death:

MARK 15:1

1 And straightway in the morning the chief priests held a consultation with the elders and scribes and the whole council, and bound Jesus, and carried him away, and delivered him to Pilate.

LUKE 22:66–71

66 And as soon as it was day, the elders of the people and the chief priests and the scribes came together, and led him into their council, saying,

67 [Chief Priests and Scribes] Art thou the Christ? tell us. And he said unto them, [Jesus] If I tell you, ye will not believe:

68 And if I also ask you, ye will not answer me, nor let me go.

69 Hereafter shall the Son of man sit on the right hand of the power of God.

70 Then said they all, [Chief Priests and Scribes] Art thou then the Son of God? And he said unto them, [Jesus] Ye say that I am.

71 And they said, [Chief Priests and Scribes] What need we any further witness? for we ourselves have heard of his own mouth.

JOHN 18:24, 28

24 Now Annas had sent him bound unto Caiaphas the high priest.

28 Then led they Jesus from Caiaphas unto the hall of judgment: and it was early; and they themselves went not into the judgment hall, lest they should be defiled; but that they might eat the passover.

64

HEARING BEFORE PILATE

MATTHEW 27:2, 11–14; MARK 15:1–5;
LUKE 23:1–6; JOHN 18:28–38
Location: Jerusalem

Summary

Luke says that after the encounter with Caiaphas, the whole multitude led Jesus to the judgment hall before Pontius Pilate,[39] who was governor over the land. They arrived early in the morning, and the chief priests, elders, and scribes did not go in, lest they become defiled. It is clear that the chief priests, elders, and scribes did not have the authority to pursue the capital punishment that they desired and had to take Jesus to Pilate.

Because Jesus' accusers did not enter the judgment hall, it appears that Pilate came out to them to inquire as to why they had brought Jesus to him. The Lord's accusers said, "We found this fellow perverting the nation, and forbidding to give tribute to Cæsar, saying that he is Christ a King" (Luke 23:2). With that, Pilate went back into the judgment hall and asked Jesus, "Are thou king of the Jews?" (verse 3).

Jesus then asked Pilot if he was inquiring for himself or if others were inquiring. Pilot then told Jesus that His own people (the Jews) delivered him up, and Pilot wanted to know what Jesus had done to deserve it. At this, Jesus told Pilot that His kingdom was not of this world, after which Pilot returns to the mob of Jews and tells them that he finds no fault with Jesus.

This drew a swift and fierce response from Jesus' accusers, saying, "He stirreth up the people, teaching throughout all Jewry, beginning from Galilee to this place" (verse 5). Pilate then asked if Jesus was a Galilaean.

MATTHEW 27:2, 11–14

2 And when they had bound him, they led him away, and delivered him to Pontius Pilate the governor.

11 And Jesus stood before the governor: and the governor asked him, saying, [**Pontius Pilate**] **Art thou the King of the Jews?** And Jesus said unto him, [**Jesus**] **Thou sayest.**

12 And when he was accused of the chief priests and elders, he answered nothing.

13 Then said Pilate unto him, [**Pilate**] **Hearest thou not how many things they witness against thee?**

14 And he answered him to never a word; insomuch that the governor marvelled greatly.

MARK 15:1–5

1 And straightway in the morning the chief priests held a consultation with the elders and scribes and the whole council, and bound Jesus, and carried him away, and delivered him to Pilate.

2 And Pilate asked him, [**Pilate**] **Art thou the King of the Jews?** And he answering said unto him, [**Jesus**] **Thou sayest it.**

3 And the chief priests accused him of many things: but he answered nothing.

4 And Pilate asked him again, saying, [**Pilate**] **Answerest thou nothing? behold how many things they witness against thee.**

5 But Jesus yet answered nothing; so that Pilate marvelled.

LUKE 23:1–6

1 And the whole multitude of them arose, and led him unto Pilate.

2 And they began to accuse him, saying, [**Whole Multitude**] **We found this fellow perverting the nation, and**

forbidding to give tribute to Cæsar, saying that he himself is Christ a King.

3 And Pilate asked him, saying, [Pilate] **Art thou the King of the Jews?** And he answered him and said, [Jesus] **Thou sayest it.**

4 Then said Pilate to the chief priests and to the people, [Pilate] **I find no fault in this man.**

5 And they were the more fierce, saying, [Chief Priests] **He stirreth up the people, teaching throughout all Jewry, beginning from Galilee to this place.**

6 When Pilate heard of Galilee, he asked whether the man were a Galilæan.

JOHN 18:28–38

28 Then led they Jesus from Caiaphas unto the hall of judgment: and it was early; and they themselves went not into the judgment hall, lest they should be defiled; but that they might eat the passover.

29 Pilate then went out unto them, and said, [Pilate] **What accusation bring ye against this man?**

30 They answered and said unto him, [Multitude] **If he were not a malefactor, we would not have delivered him up unto thee.**

31 Then said Pilate unto them, [Pilate] **Take ye him, and judge him according to your law.** The Jews therefore said unto him, [Jews] **It is not lawful for us to put any man to death:**

32 That the saying of Jesus might be fulfilled, which he spake, signifying what death he should die.

33 Then Pilate entered into the judgment hall again, and called Jesus, and said unto him, [Pilate] **Art thou the King of the Jews?**

34 Jesus answered him, [Jesus] **Sayest thou this thing of thyself, or did others tell it thee of me?**

35 Pilate answered, [Pilate] **Am I a Jew? Thine own nation and the chief priests have delivered thee unto me: what hast thou done?**

36 Jesus answered, [Jesus] My kingdom is not of this world: if my kingdom were of this world, then would my servants fight, that I should not be delivered to the Jews: but now is my kingdom not from hence.

37 Pilate therefore said unto him, [Pilate] Art thou a king then? Jesus answered, [Jesus] Thou sayest that I am a king. To this end was I born, and for this cause came I into the world, that I should bear witness unto the truth. Every one that is of the truth heareth my voice.

38 Pilate saith unto him, [Pilate] What is truth? And when he had said this, he went out again unto the Jews, and saith unto them, [Pilate] I find in him no fault at all.

65

JUDAS'S REMORSE
AND DEATH

MATTHEW 27:3–10
Location: Jerusalem

Summary

After Jesus was condemned to death, Judas must have started feeling very guilty and realized what he had done by betraying the Lord. He went to the chief priests and elders to return the thirty pieces of silver, but they would not take it back. Therefore, Judas threw it down on the floor of the temple and went out and hanged himself. What a powerful example of an individual making a horrible mistake. Because of the drastic step that Judas took by killing himself, it appears as if his judgment was temporarily impaired before betraying the Savior. Satan uses this same technique when tempting us today. Somehow Judas did not see the full ramifications of his acts, for when he was tempted with the money and perhaps with the acceptance of the chief priest and elders, his judgment was clouded and he fell—and the fall thereof was great.

What can we learn from this? First, I believe that each of us must continually be on our guard by praying that we won't be deceived and tempted. Second, we must be mature enough to realize our actions have ramifications that we may not like in the end. In short, we can't be so focused on the quick, temporary gain or pleasure that we sell our soul for thirty pieces of silver.

However, unlike Judas, we can repent and become clean again because of the Atonement of Jesus Christ. What a wonderful blessing this is.

MATTHEW 27:3–10

3 Then Judas, which had betrayed him, when he saw that he was condemned, repented himself, and brought again the thirty pieces of silver to the chief priests and elders,

4 Saying, [**Judas**] **I have sinned in that I have betrayed the innocent blood.** And they said, [**Jews**] **What is that to us? see thou to that.**

5 And he cast down the pieces of silver in the temple, and departed, and went and hanged himself.

6 And the chief priests took the silver pieces, and said, It is not lawful for to put them into the treasury, because it is the price of blood.

7 And they took counsel, and bought with them the potter's field, to bury strangers in.

8 Wherefore that field was called, The field of blood, unto this day.

9 Then was fulfilled that which was spoken by Jeremy the prophet, saying, And they took the thirty pieces of silver, the price of him that was valued, whom they of the children of Israel did value;

10 And gave them for the potter's field, as the Lord appointed me.

66

HEARING BEFORE HEROD

LUKE 23:7–12
Location: Jerusalem

Summary

As soon as Pilate discovered that Jesus was a Galilean and realized that He fell under the jurisdiction of Herod, he sent Jesus to Herod, who happened to be in Jerusalem at the time. Upon seeing Jesus, Herod was glad because he had heard about Jesus and some of the miracles that He had performed and wanted to see some of the miracles himself. When Herod questioned Jesus, Jesus did not respond. However, the chief priests and scribes did respond and "vehemently accused him" (Luke 23:10). The Lord's lack of response coupled with the chief priests' accusations caused Herod to dismiss Jesus and send Him back to Pilate. Before doing so, however, the soldiers mocked the Lord and put on Him a "gorgeous robe" (verse 11) to humiliate the Savior and make fun of Him.

LUKE 23:7–12

7 And as soon as he knew that he belonged unto Herod's jurisdiction, he sent him to Herod, who himself also was at Jerusalem at that time.

8 And when Herod saw Jesus, he was exceeding glad: for he was desirous to see him of a long season, because he

had heard many things of him; and he hoped to have seen some miracle done by him.

9 Then he questioned with him in many words; but he answered him nothing.

10 And the chief priests and scribes stood and vehemently accused him.

11 And Herod with his men of war set him at nought, and mocked him, and arrayed him in a gorgeous robe, and sent him again to Pilate.

12 And the same day Pilate and Herod were made friends together: for before they were at enmity between themselves.

67

SECOND HEARING
BEFORE PILATE

MATTHEW 27:15–31; MARK 15:6–15;
LUKE 23:11–17
Location: Jerusalem

Summary

After Herod sent Jesus back to Pilate because he could find no wrongdoing with Him, Pilate offered to release a prisoner in His stead. This act was customary during the Feast of the Passover. At this time there was a notable prisoner accused of murder named Barabbas. Pilate asked the multitude (chief priests, elders, and scribes), "Whom will ye that I release unto you? Barabbas, or Jesus which is called Christ? For he knew that for envy they had delivered him" (Matthew 27:17–18). This last sentence suggests that Pilate knew that the accusations against Jesus had no merit.

Pilate's wife sent him a message that he should have nothing to do with Jesus, for He was a just man and she had suffered in a dream because of Him. When Pilate offered the mob the option between Barabbas and Jesus, they asked him to release Barabbas. Pilate then asked them what he should do with Jesus. They said, "Let him be crucified" (verse 22). Pilate responded by asking, "Why, what evil hath he done?" But they shouted out more, saying, "Let him be crucified" (verse 23). The mob was unwilling to accept Barabbas. They were intent on crucifying Jesus and were becoming more vehement in their demands. Pilate took water and washed his hands before them, saying, "I am innocent of the blood of this just person: see ye to it. Then answered all the people, and said, His blood be on us, and on our children" (verses 24–25).

At that point, Pilate released Barabbas. The soldiers stripped Jesus of His clothes, scourged Him, clothed Him in a scarlet robe, put a plaited crown of thorns on His head, and put a reed in His hand. Then they bowed before Him, mocking Him, and said, "Hail, King of the Jews" (verse 29). They spat upon Him and smote Him on the head with the reed. After these acts, they took off the robe and returned His garments and led Him away to be crucified.

MATTHEW 27:15–31

15 Now at that feast the governor was wont to release unto the people a prisoner, whom they would.

16 And they had then a notable prisoner, called Barabbas.

17 Therefore when they were gathered together, Pilate said unto them, [Pilate] **Whom will ye that I release unto you? Barabbas, or Jesus which is called Christ?**

18 For he knew that for envy they had delivered him.

19 When he was set down on the judgment seat, his wife sent unto him, saying, [Pilate's Wife] **Have thou nothing to do with that just man: for I have suffered many things this day in a dream because of him.**

20 But the chief priests and elders persuaded the multitude that they should ask Barabbas, and destroy Jesus.

21 The governor answered and said unto them, [Pilate] **Whether of the twain will ye that I release unto you?** They said, [Jews] **Barabbas.**

22 Pilate saith unto them, [Pilate] **What shall I do then with Jesus which is called Christ?** They all say unto him, [Jews] **Let him be crucified.**

23 And the governor said, [Pilate] **Why, what evil hath he done?** But they cried out the more, saying, [Jews] **Let him be crucified.**

24 When Pilate saw that he could prevail nothing, but that rather a tumult was made, he took water, and washed

his hands before the multitude, saying, [**Pilate**] **I am innocent of the blood of this just person: see ye to it.**

25 Then answered all the people, and said, [**Jews**] **His blood be on us, and on our children.**

26 Then released he Barabbas unto them: and when he had scourged Jesus, he delivered him to be crucified.

27 Then the soldiers of the governor took Jesus into the common hall, and gathered unto him the whole band of soldiers.

28 And they stripped him, and put on him a scarlet robe.

29 And when they had plaited a crown of thorns, they put it upon his head, and a reed in his right hand: and they bowed the knee before him, and mocked him, saying, [**Soldiers**] **Hail, King of the Jews!**

30 And they spit upon him, and took the reed, and smote him on the head.

31 And after that they had mocked him, they took the robe off from him, and put his own raiment on him, and led him away to crucify him.

MARK 15:6–15

6 Now at that feast he released unto them one prisoner, whomsoever they desired.

7 And there was one named Barabbas, which lay bound with them that had made insurrection with him, who had committed murder in the insurrection.

8 And the multitude crying aloud began to desire him to do as he had ever done unto them.

9 But Pilate answered them, saying, [**Pilate**] **Will ye that I release unto you the King of the Jews?**

10 For he knew that the chief priests had delivered him for envy.

11 But the chief priests moved the people, that he should rather release Barabbas unto them.

12 And Pilate answered and said again unto them, [**Pilate**] **What will ye then that I shall do unto him whom ye call the King of the Jews?**

13 And they cried out again, [Jews] **Crucify him.**

14 Then Pilate said unto them, [Pilate] **Why, what evil hath he done?** And they cried out the more exceedingly, [Jews] **Crucify him.**

15 And so Pilate, willing to content the people, released Barabbas unto them, and delivered Jesus, when he had scourged him, to be crucified.

LUKE 23:11–17

11 And Herod with his men of war set him at nought, and mocked him, and arrayed him in a gorgeous robe, and sent him again to Pilate.

12 And the same day Pilate and Herod were made friends together: for before they were at enmity between themselves.

13 And Pilate, when he had called together the chief priests and the rulers and the people,

14 Said unto them, [Pilate] **Ye have brought this man unto me, as one that perverteth the people: and, behold, I, having examined him before you, have found no fault in this man touching those things whereof ye accuse him:**

15 **No, nor yet Herod: for I sent you to him; and, lo, nothing worthy of death is done unto him.**

16 **I will therefore chastise him, and release him.**

17 (For of necessity he must release one unto them at the feast.)

68

A MURDERER RELEASED

MATTHEW 27:15–21, 26; MARK 15:6–15;
LUKE 23:18–25; JOHN 18:39–40
Location: Jerusalem

Summary

See the summary in section 67. Note that in Luke's version of the events, Barabbas is referred to as a murderer, whereas in John's version he is referred to as a robber.

MATTHEW 27:15–21, 26
See scriptures in the previous section.

MARK 15:6–15
See scriptures in the previous section.

LUKE 23:18–25
18 And they cried out all at once, saying, [**Multitude**] **Away with this man, and release unto us Barabbas:**
19 (Who for a certain sedition made in the city, and for murder, was cast into prison.)
20 Pilate therefore, willing to release Jesus, spake again to them.

21 But they cried, saying, [**Multitude**] **Crucify him, crucify him.**

22 And he said unto them the third time, [**Pilate**] **Why, what evil hath he done? I have found no cause of death in him: I will therefore chastise him, and let him go.**

23 And they were instant with loud voices, requiring that he might be crucified. And the voices of them and of the chief priests prevailed.

24 And Pilate gave sentence that it should be as they required.

25 And he released unto them him that for sedition and murder was cast into prison, whom they had desired; but he delivered Jesus to their will.

JOHN 18:39–40

39 [**Pilate**] **But ye have a custom, that I should release unto you one at the passover: will ye therefore that I release unto you the King of the Jews?**

40 Then cried they all again, saying, [**Multitude**] **Not this man, but Barabbas.** Now Barabbas was a robber.

69

BLOOD GUILTINESS

MATTHEW 27:24–26; LUKE 23:4, 14, 22; JOHN 19:4
Location: Jerusalem

Summary

See the summary in section 67.

MATTHEW 27:24–26

24 When Pilate saw that he could prevail nothing, but that rather a tumult was made, he took water, and washed his hands before the multitude, saying, [**Pilate**] **I am innocent of the blood of this just person: see ye to it.**

25 Then answered all the people, and said, [**Jews**] **His blood be on us, and on our children.**

26 Then released he Barabbas unto them: and when he had scourged Jesus, he delivered him to be crucified.

LUKE 23:4, 14, 22

4 Then said Pilate to the chief priests and to the people, [**Pilate**] **I find no fault in this man.**

14 Said unto them, [**Pilate**] **Ye have brought this man unto me, as one that perverteth the people: and,**

behold, I, having examined him before you, have found no fault in this man touching those things whereof ye accuse him:

22 And he said unto them the third time, [Pilate] Why, what evil hath he done? I have found no cause of death in him: I will therefore chastise him, and let him go.

JOHN 19:4

4 Pilate therefore went forth again, and saith unto them, [Pilate] Behold, I bring him forth to you, that ye may know that I find no fault in him.

70

JESUS SCOURGED
AND MOCKED

MATTHEW 27:27–31; MARK 15:15–20;
JOHN 19:1–12; 1 NEPHI 19:9
Location: Jerusalem

Summary

In addition to the summaries in sections 67 and 68, John provides a little more insight into Pilate's last acts. It appears that Pilate was trying to convince the Jews to release Jesus. He went so far as to have the soldiers scourge the Lord and allow the soldiers to put a crown of thorns on His head, a purple robe on His body, a reed in His hand, and then mock Him and hit Him with their hands and the reed. No doubt, Jesus was a bloody mess from these actions, and it appears that Pilate was saying to the Jews, "Isn't this enough?" But they were still not content.

They cried out, "Crucify him, crucify him." The Jews indicated that Jesus ought to die because "he made himself the Son of God" (John 19:7). At this Pilate returned to the judgment hall where he kept the Lord and asked Jesus if He claimed to be the Son of God. Jesus did not respond. This upset Pilate, who then said to Jesus, "Speakest thou not to me? Knowest thou not that I have power to crucify thee, and have power to release thee?" The Lord said, "Thou couldest have no power at all against me, except it were given thee from above: therefore, he that delivered me unto thee hath the greater sin" (verses 10–11). At this, Pilate sought the Jews to release Him again, but they said, "If thou let this man go, thou art not Caesar's friend: whosoever maketh himself a king speaketh against Caesar" (verse 12). This cry from the Jews put tremendous pressure on Pilate because he knew that sedition to Caesar would cause him problems. Therefore, he capitulated and allowed the Jews to take the Lord away and be crucified.

MATTHEW 27:27–31

27 Then the soldiers of the governor took Jesus into the common hall, and gathered unto him the whole band of soldiers.

28 And they stripped him, and put on him a scarlet robe.

29 And when they had plaited a crown of thorns, they put it upon his head, and a reed in his right hand: and they bowed the knee before him, and mocked him, saying, [Soldiers] **Hail, King of the Jews!**

30 And they spit upon him, and took the reed, and smote him on the head.

31 And after that they had mocked him, they took the robe off from him, and put his own raiment on him, and led him away to crucify him.

MARK 15:15–20

15 And so Pilate, willing to content the people, released Barabbas unto them, and delivered Jesus, when he had scourged him, to be crucified.

16 And the soldiers led him away into the hall, called Prætorium; and they call together the whole band.

17 And they clothed him with purple, and plaited a crown of thorns, and put it about his head,

18 And began to salute him, [Soldiers] **Hail, King of the Jews!**

19 And they smote him on the head with a reed, and did spit upon him, and bowing their knees worshipped him.

20 And when they had mocked him, they took off the purple from him, and put his own clothes on him, and led him out to crucify him.

JOHN 19:1–12

1 Then Pilate therefore took Jesus, and scourged him.

2 And the soldiers plaited a crown of thorns, and put it on his head, and they put on him a purple robe,

3 And said, [**Soldiers**] **Hail, King of the Jews!** and they smote him with their hands.

4 Pilate therefore went forth again, and saith unto them, [**Pilate**] **Behold, I bring him forth to you, that ye may know that I find no fault in him.**

5 Then came Jesus forth, wearing the crown of thorns, and the purple robe. And Pilate saith unto them, [**Pilate**] **Behold the man!**

6 When the chief priests therefore and officers saw him, they cried out, saying, [**Chief Priests and officers**] **Crucify him, crucify him.** Pilate saith unto them, [**Pilate**] **Take ye him, and crucify him: for I find no fault in him.**

7 The Jews answered him, [**Jews**] **We have a law, and by our law he ought to die, because he made himself the Son of God.**

8 When Pilate therefore heard that saying, he was the more afraid;

9 And went again into the judgment hall, and saith unto Jesus, [**Pilate**] **Whence art thou?** But Jesus gave him no answer.

10 Then saith Pilate unto him, [**Pilate**] **Speakest thou not unto me? knowest thou not that I have power to crucify thee, and have power to release thee?**

11 Jesus answered, [**Jesus**] **Thou couldest have no power at all against me, except it were given thee from above: therefore he that delivered me unto thee hath the greater sin.**

12 And from thenceforth Pilate sought to release him: but the Jews cried out, saying, [**Jews**] **If thou let this man go, thou art not Cæsar's friend: whosoever maketh himself a king speaketh against Cæsar.**

9 And the world, because of their iniquity, shall judge him to be a thing of naught; wherefore they scourge him, and he suffereth it; and they smite him, and he suffereth it. Yea, they spit upon him, and he suffereth it, because of his loving kindness and his long-suffering towards the children of men.

71

JESUS TAKEN TO GOLGOTHA

MATTHEW 27:32–34; MARK 15:20–23;
LUKE 23:26–31; JOHN 19:13–17
Location: Near Jerusalem

Summary

After Pilate excused Jesus and those who sought to crucify Him, the soldiers compelled a man named Simon to carry the Lord's cross to Golgotha, also known as the place of the skull. Some people accompanied the Lord to Golgotha, including women who bewailed and lamented Him. The Lord turned and said to them, "Daughters of Jerusalem, weep not for me, but weep for yourselves, and for your children. For, behold, the days are coming, in the which they shall say, blessed are the barren, and the wombs that never bare, and the paps which never gave suck. Then shall they begin to say to the mountains, fall on us; and to the hills, Cover us. For if they do these things in a green tree, what shall be done in the dry" (Luke 23:28–31)?

With these words the Lord was prophesying about the horrible destruction and scattering of Israel that was forthcoming.

In writing about this, James E. Talmage said,

It was the Lord's last testimony of the impending holocaust of destruction that was to follow the nation's rejection of her King. Although motherhood was the glory of every Jewish woman's life, yet in the terrible scenes which many of those there weeping would live to witness, barrenness would be accounted a blessing; for the childless would have fewer to weep over, and at least would be spared the horror of seeing their offspring die of starvation or by violence; for so dreadful would be that day that people would fain welcome the falling of the mountains upon them to end their sufferings. If Israel's oppressors could do what was then in the process of doing to the "Green Tree," who bore the leafage of freedom and truth and offered the priceless fruit of life eternal, what would the powers of evil not do to the withered branches and dried trunk of apostate Judaism?[40]

Elder Talmage's book was written before World War II and did not consider the horrible holocaust of the Jews that took place at the hands of the Germans, which is another account of the terrible suffering that would occur to the Jewish people.

Once the company arrived at Golgotha, the soldiers gave the Lord vinegar to drink mingled with gall or myrrh. It must have tasted horrible because when the Lord tasted it He refused to drink it.

MATTHEW 27:32–34

32 And as they came out, they found a man of Cyrene, Simon by name: him they compelled to bear his cross.

33 And when they were come unto a place called Golgotha, that is to say, a place of a skull,

34 They gave him vinegar to drink mingled with gall: and when he had tasted thereof, he would not drink.

MARK 15:20–23

20 And when they had mocked him, they took off the purple from him, and put his own clothes on him, and led him out to crucify him.

21 And they compel one Simon a Cyrenian, who passed by, coming out of the country, the father of Alexander and Rufus, to bear his cross.

22 And they bring him unto the place Golgotha, which is, being interpreted, The place of a skull.

23 And they gave him to drink wine mingled with myrrh: but he received it not.

LUKE 23:26–31

26 And as they led him away, they laid hold upon one Simon, a Cyrenian, coming out of the country, and on him they laid the cross, that he might bear it after Jesus.

27 And there followed him a great company of people, and of women, which also bewailed and lamented him.

28 But Jesus turning unto them said, [**Jesus**] **Daughters of Jerusalem, weep not for me, but weep for yourselves, and for your children.**

29 **For, behold, the days are coming, in the which they shall say, Blessed are the barren, and the wombs that never bare, and the paps which never gave suck.**

30 **Then shall they begin to say to the mountains, Fall on us; and to the hills, Cover us.**

31 **For if they do these things in a green tree, what shall be done in the dry?**

JOHN 19:13–17

13 When Pilate therefore heard that saying, he brought Jesus forth, and sat down in the judgment seat in a place that is called the Pavement, but in the Hebrew, Gabbatha.

14 And it was the preparation of the passover, and about the sixth hour: and he saith unto the Jews, [**Pilate**] **Behold your King!**

15 But they cried out, [**Jews**] **Away with him, away with him, crucify him.** Pilate saith unto them, [**Pilate**] **Shall I crucify your King?** The chief priests answered, [**Chief Priests**] **We have no king but Cæsar.**

16 Then delivered he him therefore unto them to be crucified. And they took Jesus, and led him away.

17 And he bearing his cross went forth into a place called the place of a skull, which is called in the Hebrew Golgotha:

72

THE CRUCIFIXION

MATTHEW 27:35–44; MARK 15:24–33;
LUKE 23:32–43; JOHN 19:18–22;
HELAMAN 14:20–27; 3 NEPHI 8:5–22; 10:9
Location: Golgotha

Summary

Once the party arrived at Golgotha (Luke says Calvary), the soldiers crucified the Lord and cast lots for His garments, which was a fulfillment of prophecy. Stripping a prisoner of his garments is another form of torture because of the humiliation that accompanies it. After casting lots for His garments, the soldiers put a sign above His head that said, "THIS IS JESUS THE KING OF THE JEWS" (Matthew 27:37. See pages 191–92 for the other Gospel authors' interpretation of the sign.) Then they sat down to watch Him. On both sides of Him were two thieves crucified at the same time. These acts were all done at about the third hour. While on the cross, the Lord said, "Father, forgive them; for they know not what they do" (Luke 23:34).

Over the next six hours, the chief priests, scribes, elders, and others came and "passed by," reviling Him and wagging their heads while saying, "Thou that destroyest the temple, and buildest it in three days, save thyself. If thou be the Son of God, come down from the cross" (Matthew 27:40). They justified their actions by saying, "He saved others; himself he cannot save. If he be the King of Israel, let him come down from the cross, and we will believe him. He trusted in God; let him deliver him now, if he will have him: for he said, I am the Son of God" (verses 42–43).

Even one of the thieves next to the Lord leveled the same accusations at Him. However, the other thief pointed out that they (meaning the thieves) deserved what they were getting, but the Lord had done nothing to deserve this. This particular thief requested of the Lord, "Remember me when thou comest into thy kingdom" (Luke 42:32). The Lord replied, "To day shalt thou be with me in paradise" (verse 33).

At the sixth hour, which would be the midpoint of the crucifixion, darkness covered the land. It lasted three hours. Although not stated explicitly, there is no indication that there was complete darkness like that experienced in the land of the Nephites. This darkness may have been similar to the darkness that occurs when with a bad storm. Helaman prophesied in the Book of Mormon that a sign of the Savior's death would be great destruction in the land followed by three days of darkness until the Savior rose from the dead (see 3 Nephi 8).

MATTHEW 27:35–44

35 And they crucified him, and parted his garments, casting lots: that it might be fulfilled which was spoken by the prophet, They parted my garments among them, and upon my vesture did they cast lots.

36 And sitting down they watched him there;

37 And set up over his head his accusation written, THIS IS JESUS THE KING OF THE JEWS.

38 Then were there two thieves crucified with him, one on the right hand, and another on the left.

39 And they that passed by reviled him, wagging their heads,

40 And saying, [Multitude] **Thou that destroyest the temple, and buildest it in three days, save thyself. If thou be the Son of God, come down from the cross.**

41 Likewise also the chief priests mocking him, with the scribes and elders, said,

42 [Chief Priests, Scribes, and Elders] **He saved others; himself he cannot save. If he be the King of Israel, let him now come down from the cross, and we will believe him.**

43 He trusted in God; let him deliver him now, if he will have him: for he said, I am the Son of God.

44 The thieves also, which were crucified with him, casteth same in his teeth.

MARK 15:24–33

24 And when they had crucified him, they parted his garments, casting lots upon them, what every man should take.

25 And it was the third hour, and they crucified him.

26 And the superscription of his accusation was written over, THE KING OF THE JEWS.

27 And with him they crucify two thieves; the one on his right hand, and the other on his left.

28 And the scripture was fulfilled, which saith, And he was numbered with the transgressors.

29 And they that passed by railed on him, wagging their heads, and saying, **[Passerby's]** **Ah, thou that destroyest the temple, and buildest it in three days,**

30 Save thyself, and come down from the cross.

31 Likewise also the chief priests mocking said among themselves with the scribes, **[Chief Priests and Scribes]** **He saved others; himself he cannot save.**

32 Let Christ the King of Israel descend now from the cross, that we may see and believe. And they that were crucified with him reviled him.

33 And when the sixth hour was come, there was darkness over the whole land until the ninth hour.

LUKE 23:32–43

32 And there were also two other, malefactors, led with him to be put to death.

33 And when they were come to the place, which is called Calvary, there they crucified him, and the malefactors, one on the right hand, and the other on the left.

34 Then said Jesus, **[Jesus]** **Father, forgive them; for they know not what they do.** And they parted his raiment, and cast lots.

35 And the people stood beholding. And the rulers also with them derided him, saying, [**Rulers**] **He saved others; let him save himself, if he be Christ, the chosen of God.**

36 And the soldiers also mocked him, coming to him, and offering him vinegar,

37 And saying, [**Soldiers**] **If thou be the king of the Jews, save thyself.**

38 And a superscription also was written over him in letters of Greek, and Latin, and Hebrew, THIS IS THE KING OF THE JEWS.

39 And one of the malefactors which were hanged railed on him, saying, [**Malefactor**] **If thou be Christ, save thyself and us.**

40 But the other answering rebuked him, saying, [**Other Malefactor**] **Dost not thou fear God, seeing thou art in the same condemnation?**

41 **And we indeed justly; for we receive the due reward of our deeds: but this man hath done nothing amiss.**

42 And he said unto Jesus, [**Other Malefactor**] **Lord, remember me when thou comest into thy kingdom.**

43 And Jesus said unto him, [**Jesus**] **Verily I say unto thee, To day shalt thou be with me in paradise.**

JST, LUKE 23:35

Compare Luke 23:34.

Jesus asks forgiveness for the Roman soldiers who are crucifying Him.

35 Then said Jesus, Father, forgive them; for they know not what they do (Meaning the soldiers who crucified him,) and they parted his raiment and cast lots.

JOHN 19:18–22

18 Where they crucified him, and two other with him, on either side one, and Jesus in the midst.

19 And Pilate wrote a title, and put it on the cross. And the writing was, JESUS OF NAZARETH THE KING OF THE JEWS.

20 This title then read many of the Jews: for the place where Jesus was crucified was nigh to the city: and it was written in Hebrew, and Greek, and Latin.

21 Then said the chief priests of the Jews to Pilate, [Chief Priest] Write not, The King of the Jews; but that he said, I am King of the Jews.

22 Pilate answered, [Pilate] What I have written I have written.

HELAMAN 14:20–27

20 [Helaman] But behold, as I said unto you concerning another sign, a sign of his death, behold, in that day that he shall suffer death the sun shall be darkened and refuse to give his light unto you; and also the moon and the stars; and there shall be no light upon the face of this land, even from the time that he shall suffer death, for the space of three days, to the time that he shall rise again from the dead.

21 Yea, at the time that he shall yield up the ghost there shall be thunderings and lightnings for the space of many hours, and the earth shall shake and tremble; and the rocks which are upon the face of this earth, which are both above the earth and beneath, which ye know at this time are solid, or the more part of it is one solid mass, shall be broken up;

22 Yea, they shall be rent in twain, and shall ever after be found in seams and in cracks, and in broken fragments upon the face of the whole earth, yea, both above the earth and beneath.

23 And behold, there shall be great tempests, and there shall be many mountains laid low, like unto a valley, and there shall be many places which are now called valleys which shall become mountains, whose height is great.

24 And many highways shall be broken up, and many cities shall become desolate.

25 And many graves shall be opened, and shall yield up many of their dead; and many saints shall appear unto many.

26 And behold, thus hath the angel spoken unto me; for he said unto me that there should be thunderings and lightnings for the space of many hours.

27 And he said unto me that while the thunder and the lightning lasted, and the tempest, that these things should be, and that darkness should cover the face of the whole earth for the space of three days.

3 NEPHI 8:5–22

5 And it came to pass in the thirty and fourth year, in the first month, on the fourth day of the month, there arose a great storm, such an one as never had been known in all the land.

6 And there was also a great and terrible tempest; and there was terrible thunder, insomuch that it did shake the whole earth as if it was about to divide asunder.

7 And there were exceedingly sharp lightnings, such as never had been known in all the land.

8 And the city of Zarahemla did take fire.

9 And the city of Moroni did sink into the depths of the sea, and the inhabitants thereof were drowned.

10 And the earth was carried up upon the city of Moronihah, that in the place of the city there became a great mountain.

11 And there was a great and terrible destruction in the land southward.

12 But behold, there was a more great and terrible destruction in the land northward; for behold, the whole face of the land was changed, because of the tempest and the whirlwinds, and the thunderings and the lightnings, and the exceedingly great quaking of the whole earth;

13 And the highways were broken up, and the level roads were spoiled, and many smooth places became rough.

14 And many great and notable cities were sunk, and many were burned, and many were shaken till

the buildings thereof had fallen to the earth, and the inhabitants thereof were slain, and the places were left desolate.

15 And there were some cities which remained; but the damage thereof was exceedingly great, and there were many in them who were slain.

16 And there were some who were carried away in the whirlwind; and whither they went no man knoweth, save they know that they were carried away.

17 And thus the face of the whole earth became deformed, because of the tempests, and the thunderings, and the lightnings, and the quaking of the earth.

18 And behold, the rocks were rent in twain; they were broken up upon the face of the whole earth, insomuch that they were found in broken fragments, and in seams and in cracks, upon all the face of the land.

19 And it came to pass that when the thunderings, and the lightnings, and the storm, and the tempest, and the quakings of the earth did cease—for behold, they did last for about the space of three hours; and it was said by some that the time was greater; nevertheless, all these great and terrible things were done in about the space of three hours—and then behold, there was darkness upon the face of the land.

20 And it came to pass that there was thick darkness upon all the face of the land, insomuch that the inhabitants thereof who had not fallen could feel the vapor of darkness;

21 And there could be no light, because of the darkness, neither candles, neither torches; neither could there be fire kindled with their fine and exceedingly dry wood, so that there could not be any light at all;

22 And there was not any light seen, neither fire, nor glimmer, neither the sun, nor the moon, nor the stars, for so great were the mists of darkness which were upon the face of the land.

9 And it came to pass that thus did the three days pass away. And it was in the morning, and the darkness dispersed from off the face of the land, and the earth did cease to tremble, and the rocks did cease to rend, and the dreadful groanings did cease, and all the tumultuous noises did pass away.

73

SOLDIERS CAST LOTS FOR JESUS' GARMENTS

MATTHEW 27:35; MARK 15:24;
LUKE 23:34; JOHN 19:23–24
Location: Golgotha

Summary

See the summary regarding the parting of the Lord's garments in section 72.

MATTHEW 27:35

35 And they crucified him, and parted his garments, casting lots: that it might be fulfilled which was spoken by the prophet, They parted my garments among them, and upon my vesture did they cast lots.

MARK 15:24

24 And when they had crucified him, they parted his garments, casting lots upon them, what every man should take.

LUKE 23:34

34 Then said Jesus, [**Jesus**] **Father, forgive them; for they know not what they do.** And they parted his raiment, and cast lots.

JOHN 19:23-24

23 Then the soldiers, when they had crucified Jesus, took his garments, and made four parts, to every soldier a part; and also his coat: now the coat was without seam, woven from the top throughout.

24 They said therefore among themselves, [**Soldiers**] **Let us not rend it, but cast lots for it, whose it shall be:** that the scripture might be fulfilled, which saith, [**Jesus**] **They parted my raiment among them, and for my vesture they did cast lots.** These things therefore the soldiers did.

74

THE SIGN: KING OF THE JEWS

MATTHEW 27:37; MARK 15:26;
LUKE 23:38; JOHN 19:19–22
Location: Golgotha

Summary

See the summary and comments regarding the sign on the Lord's cross in section 72.

MATTHEW 27:37
37 And set up over his head his accusation written, THIS IS JESUS THE KING OF THE JEWS.

MARK 15:26
26 And the superscription of his accusation was written over, THE KING OF THE JEWS.

LUKE 23:38
38 And a superscription also was written over him in letters of Greek, and Latin, and Hebrew, THIS IS THE KING OF THE JEWS.

JOHN 19:19–22

19 And Pilate wrote a title, and put it on the cross. And the writing was, JESUS OF NAZARETH THE KING OF THE JEWS.

20 This title then read many of the Jews: for the place where Jesus was crucified was nigh to the city: and it was written in Hebrew, and Greek, and Latin.

21 Then said the chief priests of the Jews to Pilate, **[Jews] Write not, The King of the Jews; but that he said, I am King of the Jews.**

22 Pilate answered, **[Pilate] What I have written I have written.**

75

JESUS SPEAKS TO HIS MOTHER

JOHN 19:25–27
Location: Golgotha

Summary

John records that three women, including the Savior's mother, Mary, remained with the Lord during His time on the cross. Toward the end Jesus saw John the Beloved near His mother and invited John to care for her as if she were his mother. Likewise, He invited Mary to go with John as if he were her son. His concern for His mother during this time of excruciating suffering is another example of the Lord's extraordinary capacity to love and to look after those He cared for.

JOHN 19:25–27

25 Now there stood by the cross of Jesus his mother, and his mother's sister, Mary the wife of Cleophas, and Mary Magdalene.

26 When Jesus therefore saw his mother, and the disciple standing by, whom he loved, he saith unto his mother, [Jesus] **Woman, behold thy son!**

27 Then saith he to the disciple, [Jesus] **Behold thy mother!** And from that hour that disciple took her unto his own home.

76

DARKNESS: SIXTH TO NINTH HOUR

MATTHEW 27:45; MARK 15:33–36;
LUKE 23:44–45

Location: Jerusalem

Summary

Three of the Gospel authors pointed out that there was darkness in the land for three hours between the sixth and ninth hour. Luke points out that during this time the veil of the temple was rent.

MATTHEW 27:45

45 Now from the sixth hour there was darkness over all the land unto the ninth hour.

MARK 15:33–36

33 And when the sixth hour was come, there was darkness over the whole land until the ninth hour.

LUKE 23:44–45

44 And it was about the sixth hour, and there was a darkness over all the earth until the ninth hour.

45 And the sun was darkened, and the veil of the temple was rent in the midst.

194

77

DEATH OF JESUS CHRIST

MATTHEW 27:46–50; MARK 15:37;
LUKE 23:46; JOHN 19:28–30
Location: Golgotha

Summary

At about the ninth hour, Jesus cried out, "My God, my God, why hast thou forsaken me?" (Matthew 27:46). Some thought that by doing so he calleth for Elias. One person—and we don't know who it was—quickly got a sponge and dipped it in vinegar and gave it to the Lord to drink. It appears he was trying to relieve the Lord's suffering in some small way. Some did not like this response and asked that they let Him be to see if Elias would come down and help Him. They were still in a period of mocking and unbelief. Matthew and Mark both say that the Lord cried out again with a loud voice and then gave up the ghost. Luke tells us what He cried out: "Father, into thy hands I commend my spirit" (Luke 23:46), after which John said that He bowed his head and gave up the ghost (see John 19:30).

MATTHEW 27:46–50

46 And about the ninth hour Jesus cried with a loud voice, saying, [**Jesus**] **Eli, Eli, lama sabachthani?** that is to say, My God, my God, why hast thou forsaken me?

47 Some of them that stood there, when they heard that, said, [**some that stood by**] This man calleth for Elias.

195

48 And straightway one of them ran, and took a sponge, and filled it with vinegar, and put it on a reed, and gave him to drink.

49 The rest said, [The Rest of the People] **Let be, let us see whether Elias will come to save him.**

50 Jesus, when he had cried again with a loud voice, yielded up the ghost.

MARK 15:37

34 And at the ninth hour Jesus cried with a loud voice, saying, [Jesus] **Eloi, Eloi, lama sabachthani?** which is, being interpreted, My God, my God, why hast thou forsaken me?

35 And some of them that stood by, when they heard it, said, [Some That Stood By] **Behold, he calleth Elias.**

36 And one ran and filled a sponge full of vinegar, and put it on a reed, and gave him to drink, saying, [One That Stood By] **Let alone; let us see whether Elias will come to take him down.**

37 And Jesus cried with a loud voice, and gave up the ghost.

LUKE 23:46

46 And when Jesus had cried with a loud voice, he said, [Jesus] **Father, into thy hands I commend my spirit:** and having said thus, he gave up the ghost.

JOHN 19:28–30

28 After this, Jesus knowing that all things were now accomplished, that the scripture might be fulfilled, saith, [Jesus] **I thirst.**

29 Now there was set a vessel full of vinegar: and they filled a sponge with vinegar, and put it upon hyssop, and put it to his mouth.

30 When Jesus therefore had received the vinegar, he said, [Jesus] **It is finished:** and he bowed his head, and gave up the ghost.

78

EARTHQUAKE: VEIL OF THE TEMPLE RENT

MATTHEW 27:51; MARK 15:38; LUKE 23:45
Location: Jerusalem

Summary

When the Savior died, or gave up the ghost, the veil of the temple was rent in twain. It was torn in two from top to bottom, while earthquakes took place and the sun was darkened.

MATTHEW 27:51

51 And, behold, the veil of the temple was rent in twain from the top to the bottom; and the earth did quake, and the rocks rent.

MARK 15:38

38 And the veil of the temple was rent in twain from the top to the bottom.

LUKE 23:45

45 And the sun was darkened, and the veil of the temple was rent in the midst.

79

SIDE PIERCED BY SPEAR

JOHN 19:31–34
Location: Golgotha

Summary

The Sabbath Day was quickly approaching, and Jewish law prohibited that bodies remain on crosses on that day. Therefore, the Jews asked Pilate to allow the soldiers to break the legs of those on crosses that they might be taken away. The Jews must have been successful in this request because the soldiers broke the legs of the two thieves that hung on the crosses next to Jesus. When they came to Jesus, they could see that He was already dead. Rather than break His legs, one of the soldiers pierced His side with a spear, causing blood and water to gush forth.

JOHN 19:31–34

31 The Jews therefore, because it was the preparation, that the bodies should not remain upon the cross on the sabbath day, (for that sabbath day was an high day,) besought Pilate that their legs might be broken, and that they might be taken away.

32 Then came the soldiers, and brake the legs of the first, and of the other which was crucified with him.

33 But when they came to Jesus, and saw that he was dead already, they brake not his legs:

34 But one of the soldiers with a spear pierced his side, and forthwith came there out blood and water.

80

PASSOVER SCRIPTURES FULFILLED

JOHN 19:35–37
Location: Golgotha

Summary

John notes in his account that the Passover scriptures were fulfilled when the soldiers pierced the Lord's side rather than breaking His legs.

JOHN 19:35–37

35 And he that saw it bare record, and his record is true: and he knoweth that he saith true, that ye might believe.

36 For these things were done, that the scripture should be fulfilled, A bone of him shall not be broken.

37 And again another scripture saith, They shall look on him whom they pierced.

81

WATCHERS NEAR THE CROSS

MATTHEW 27:54–56; MARK 15:39–41;
LUKE 23:47–49
Location: Golgotha

Summary

When the Savior gave up the ghost, which was preceded by physical signs of darkness and earthquakes, one of the soldiers testified of the divine nature of Jesus when he said, "Truly this was the Son of God" (Matthew 27:54). The Gospel authors point out that many women were nearby watching. They were disciples of the Lord and had ministered unto Him during his mortal sojourn.

MATTHEW 27:54–56

54 Now when the centurion, and they that were with him, watching Jesus, saw the earthquake, and those things that were done, they feared greatly, saying, [**Centurion**] **Truly this was the Son of God.**

55 And many women were there beholding afar off, which followed Jesus from Galilee, ministering unto him:

56 Among which was Mary Magdalene, and Mary the mother of James and Joses, and the mother of Zebedee's children.

MARK 15:39–41

39 And when the centurion, which stood over against him, saw that he so cried out, and gave up the ghost, he said, [Centurion] **Truly this man was the Son of God.**

40 There were also women looking on afar off: among whom was Mary Magdalene, and Mary the mother of James the less and of Joses, and Salome;

41 (Who also, when he was in Galilee, followed him, and ministered unto him;) and many other women which came up with him unto Jerusalem.

LUKE 23:47–49

47 Now when the centurion saw what was done, he glorified God, saying, [Centurion] **Certainly this was a righteous man.**

48 And all the people that came together to that sight, beholding the things which were done, smote their breasts, and returned.

49 And all his acquaintance, and the women that followed him from Galilee, stood afar off, beholding these things.

82

JESUS' BURIAL

MATTHEW 27:57–61; MARK 15:42–47;
LUKE 23:50–56; JOHN 19:38–42
Location: Near Jerusalem

Summary

Because the Sabbath Day was quickly approaching and because Jesus died on the day of preparation for the Sabbath, there was a desire to take care of the body of Jesus expeditiously. Joseph of Arimathea, a disciple of Jesus and a man of wealth and status, went unto Pilate secretly, for fear of the Jews, and begged the body of Jesus. Pilate was surprised to hear that Jesus was already dead, but after verifying that He was, he released the Lord's body as requested. With that, Joseph of Arimathea bought fine linen, and with Nicodemus who had prepared spices and ointments, took the Lord's body down from the cross, wrapped it in the linen with the spices, and laid Him in his new sepulcher. This sepulcher had never been used and was hewn out of a rock. They then rolled a great stone to cover the door of the sepulcher and departed. All the while, Mary Magdalene and Mary the mother of Joses "beheld where he was laid" (Mark 15:47).

MATTHEW 27:57–61

57 When the even was come, there came a rich man of Arimathæa, named Joseph, who also himself was Jesus' disciple:

58 He went to Pilate, and begged the body of Jesus. Then Pilate commanded the body to be delivered.

59 And when Joseph had taken the body, he wrapped it in a clean linen cloth,

60 And laid it in his own new tomb, which he had hewn out in the rock: and he rolled a great stone to the door of the sepulchre, and departed.

61 And there was Mary Magdalene, and the other Mary, sitting over against the sepulchre.

MARK 15:42–47

42 And now when the even was come, because it was the preparation, that is, the day before the sabbath,

43 Joseph of Arimathæa, an honourable counsellor, which also waited for the kingdom of God, came, and went in boldly unto Pilate, and craved the body of Jesus.

44 And Pilate marvelled if he were already dead: and calling unto him the centurion, he asked him whether he had been any while dead.

45 And when he knew it of the centurion, he gave the body to Joseph.

46 And he bought fine linen, and took him down, and wrapped him in the linen, and laid him in a sepulcher which was hewn out of a rock, and rolled a stone unto the door of the sepulchre.

47 And Mary Magdalene and Mary the mother of Joses beheld where he was laid.

LUKE 23:50–56

50 And, behold, there was a man named Joseph, a counsellor; and he was a good man, and a just:

51 (The same had not consented to the counsel and deed of them;) he was of Arimathæa, a city of the Jews: who also himself waited for the kingdom of God.

52 This man went unto Pilate, and begged the body of Jesus.

53 And he took it down, and wrapped it in linen, and laid it in a sepulchre that was hewn in stone, wherein never man before was laid.

54 And that day was the preparation, and the sabbath drew on.

55 And the women also, which came with him from Galilee, followed after, and beheld the sepulchre, and how his body was laid.

56 And they returned, and prepared spices and ointments; and rested the sabbath day according to the commandment.

JOHN 19:38–42

38 And after this Joseph of Arimathæa, being a disciple of Jesus, but secretly for fear of the Jews, besought Pilate that he might take away the body of Jesus: and Pilate gave him leave. He came therefore, and took the body of Jesus.

39 And there came also Nicodemus, which at the first came to Jesus by night, and brought a mixture of myrrh and aloes, about an hundred pound weight.

40 Then took they the body of Jesus, and wound it in linen clothes with the spices, as the manner of the Jews is to bury.

41 Now in the place where he was crucified there was a garden; and in the garden a new sepulcher, wherein was never man yet laid.

42 There laid they Jesus therefore because of the Jews' preparation day; for the sepulchre was nigh at hand.

83

CHIEF PRIESTS AND PHARISEES SEAL THE TOMB

MATTHEW 27:62–66
Location: Near Jerusalem

Summary

The day after the death and burial of the Lord, chief priests and Pharisees went to Pilate and argued that Jesus had taught that three days after His death He would rise again; therefore, to prohibit His followers from stealing His body and falsely claiming that Jesus had risen from the dead, Pilot should order the sepulcher closed, sealed, and guarded (Matthew 27:63–64). At this Pilate permitted them to seal the stone door of the tomb and to set a watch, a centurion, to make sure the seal was not broken.

MATTHEW 27:62–66

62 Now the next day, that followed the day of the preparation, the chief priests and Pharisees came together unto Pilate,

63 Saying, **[Chief Priests and Pharisees] Sir, we remember that that deceiver said, while he was yet alive, After three days I will rise again.**

64 Command therefore that the sepulchre be made sure until the third day, lest his disciples come by night, and steal him away, and say unto the people, He is risen from the dead: so the last error shall be worse than the first.

65 Pilate said unto them, [Pilate] Ye have a watch: go your way, make it as sure as ye can.

66 So they went, and made the sepulchre sure, sealing the stone, and setting a watch.

84

EARTHQUAKE, ANGELS OPEN TOMB

MATTHEW 28:2–4
Location: Near Jerusalem

Summary

At some point, there was a great earthquake, and an angel of the Lord descended from heaven and came and rolled back the stone that covered the tomb. Matthew said that the angel's countenance was like lightning and his clothing as snow. The centurions shook and fell to the ground as if they were dead.

MATTHEW 28:2–4

2 And, behold, there was a great earthquake: for the angel of the Lord descended from heaven, and came and rolled back the stone from the door, and sat upon it.

3 His countenance was like lightning, and his raiment white as snow:

4 And for fear of him the keepers did shake, and became as dead men.

85

WOMEN FIND THE OPEN TOMB

MATTHEW 28:1; MARK 16:1–4;
LUKE 24:1–2; JOHN 20:1–2
Location: Near Jerusalem

Summary

The day after the Sabbath, early in the morning at the rising of the sun, Mary Magdalene, Mary the mother of James, and Salome went to the sepulcher with spices to anoint the Lord's body. While en route they said among themselves, "Who shall roll us away the stone from the door of the sepulchre?" (Mark 16:3). When they arrived, they saw that the stone had been rolled away from the entrance.

Matthew said that when they entered the sepulcher, they saw an angel sitting on the right side, clothed in a long white garment. He greeted them and told them not to fear. He knew they were there to visit the body of the Lord, but the Lord had risen. He then invited them to see the place where Jesus had lain and to go quickly and tell the disciples that the Lord had risen from the dead.

Luke provides a different account. He said, "And it came to pass, as they were much perplexed thereabout, behold, two men stood by them in shining garments: And as they were afraid, and bowed down their faces to the earth, they said unto them, Why seek ye the living among the dead? He is not here, but is risen: remember how he spake unto you when he was yet in Galilee, Saying, The Son of man must be delivered into the hands of sinful men, and be crucified, and the third day rise again. And they remembered his words" (Luke 24:4–8).

Mary Magdalene ran to Simon Peter and to the other disciple, whom Jesus loved, and said, "They have taken away the Lord out of the sepulchre, and we know not where they have laid him" (John 20:2).

MATTHEW 28:1

1 In the end of the sabbath, as it began to dawn toward the first day of the week, came Mary Magdalene and the other Mary to see the sepulchre.

MARK 16:1–4

1 And when the sabbath was past, Mary Magdalene, and Mary the mother of James, and Salome, had bought sweet spices, that they might come and anoint him.

2 And very early in the morning the first day of the week, they came unto the sepulchre at the rising of the sun.

3 And they said among themselves, [**Mary Magdalene, Mary the mother of James, and Salome**] **Who shall roll us away the stone from the door of the sepulchre?**

4 And when they looked, they saw that the stone was rolled away: for it was very great.

JST, MARK 16:3–6.

Compare Mark 16:4–7; Luke 24:2–4.
Two angels greet the women at the tomb of the Savior.

3 But when they looked, they saw that the stone was rolled away, (for it was very great,) and two angels sitting thereon, clothed in long white garments; and they were affrighted.

4 But the angels said unto them, [**Angels**] **Be not affrighted; ye seek Jesus of Nazareth, who was crucified; he is risen; he is not here; behold the place where they laid him;**

5 And go your way, tell his disciples and Peter, that he goeth before you into Galilee; there shall ye see him as he said unto you.

6 And they, entering into the sepulcher, saw the place where they laid Jesus.

LUKE 24:1–2

1 Now upon the first day of the week, very early in the morning, they came unto the sepulchre, bringing the spices which they had prepared, and certain others with them.

2 And they found the stone rolled away from the sepulchre.

JOHN 20:1–2

1 The first day of the week cometh Mary Magdalene early, when it was yet dark, unto the sepulchre, and seeth the stone taken away from the sepulchre.

2 Then she runneth, and cometh to Simon Peter, and to the other disciple, whom Jesus loved, and saith unto them, **[Mary Magdalene] They have taken away the Lord out of the sepulchre, and we know not where they have laid him.**

86

ANGELS PROCLAIM: "HE IS RISEN"

MATTHEW 28:5–7; MARK 16:5–7; LUKE 24:3–8
Location: Near Jerusalem

Summary

See the summary in section 85.

MATTHEW 28:5–7

5 And the angel answered and said unto the women, [Angel] Fear not ye: for I know that ye seek Jesus, which was crucified.

6 He is not here: for he is risen, as he said. Come, see the place where the Lord lay.

7 And go quickly, and tell his disciples that he is risen from the dead; and, behold, he goeth before you into Galilee; there shall ye see him: lo, I have told you.

MARK 16:5–7

5 And entering into the sepulchre, they saw a young man sitting on the right side, clothed in a long white garment; and they were affrighted.

6 And he saith unto them, Be not affrighted: Ye seek Jesus of Nazareth, which was crucified: he is risen; he is not here: behold the place where they laid him.

7 But go your way, tell his disciples and Peter that he goeth before you into Galilee: there shall ye see him, as he said unto you.

LUKE 24:3–8

3 And they entered in, and found not the body of the Lord Jesus.

4 And it came to pass, as they were much perplexed thereabout, behold, two men stood by them in shining garments:

5 And as they were afraid, and bowed down their faces to the earth, they said unto them, [**Two Men-Angels**] **Why seek ye the living among the dead?**

6 He is not here, but is risen: remember how he spake unto you when he was yet in Galilee,

7 Saying, The Son of man must be delivered into the hands of sinful men, and be crucified, and the third day rise again.

8 And they remembered his words,

JST, LUKE 24:2–4

Compare Luke 24:2–5.

The women see two angels at Jesus' sepulcher.

2 And they found the stone rolled away from the sepulcher, and two angels standing by it in shining garments.

3 And they entered into the sepulcher, and not finding the body of the Lord Jesus, they were much perplexed thereabout;

4 And were affrighted, and bowed down their faces to the earth. But behold the angels said unto them, Why seek ye the living among the dead?

87

WOMEN HURRY TO TELL THE APOSTLES

MATTHEW 28:8; MARK 16:8;
LUKE 24:9–11; JOHN 20:18
Location: Near Jerusalem

Summary

After encountering the angel and hearing the words that "He is not here, but is risen" (Matthew 28:6), the women departed quickly from the sepulchre and ran to tell the Apostles. They were, of course, shaken and were trembling from this experience. They did not stop to tell others.

MATTHEW 28:8

8 And they departed quickly from the sepulchre with fear and great joy; and did run to bring his disciples word.

MARK 16:8

8 And they went out quickly, and fled from the sepulchre; for they trembled and were amazed: neither said they any thing to any man; for they were afraid.

LUKE 24:9–11

9 And returned from the sepulchre, and told all these things unto the eleven, and to all the rest.

10 It was Mary Magdalene, and Joanna, and Mary the mother of James, and other women that were with them, which told these things unto the apostles.

11 And their words seemed to them as idle tales, and they believed them not.

JOHN 20:18

18 Mary Magdalene came and told the disciples that she had seen the Lord, and that he had spoken these things unto her.

88

PETER AND JOHN RUN TO THE TOMB

LUKE 24:12; JOHN 20:3–10
Location: Near Jerusalem

Summary

After the women told the Apostles what they had heard and seen, Peter and the other disciple ran to the sepulcher. The other disciple outran Peter and arrived first. He looked in and saw linen cloths, but he did not go in. Once Peter caught up and arrived at the sepulcher, he went in and saw the linen cloths and also saw the "napkin" that was about the Lord's head wrapped together by itself away from the other cloths. They must have been perplexed and didn't know what to do, so they left and went to their own homes. John writes that Mary was without the sepulcher weeping, so she must have followed them back to the sepulcher.

LUKE 24:12

12 Then arose Peter, and ran unto the sepulchre; and stooping down, he beheld the linen clothes laid by themselves, and departed, wondering in himself at that which was come to pass.

215

3 Peter therefore went forth, and that other disciple, and came to the sepulchre.

4 So they ran both together: and the other disciple did outrun Peter, and came first to the sepulchre.

5 And he stooping down, and looking in, saw the linen clothes lying; yet went he not in.

6 Then cometh Simon Peter following him, and went into the sepulchre, and seeth the linen clothes lie,

7 And the napkin, that was about his head, not lying with the linen clothes, but wrapped together in a place by itself.

8 Then went in also that other disciple, which came first to the sepulchre, and he saw, and believed.

9 For as yet they knew not the scripture, that he must rise again from the dead.

10 Then the disciples went away again unto their own home.

11 But Mary stood without at the sepulchre weeping: and as she wept, she stooped down, and looked into the sepulchre,

89

JESUS APPEARS TO MARY MAGDALENE

MARK 16:9–11; JOHN 20:11–18
Location: Near Jerusalem

Summary

Early in the morning on the first day of the week (Sunday), Mary Magdalene was outside the sepulcher weeping. She stooped down and looked in and saw two angels sitting where Jesus had laid. They asked her why she was weeping, and she told them that someone had taken away the body of her Lord and she didn't know where they had laid Him. At that point, she must have felt or seen someone come up behind her and turned back to see who it was, but she didn't recognize that it was the Lord. Jesus asked her, "Why weepest thou? Who seekest thou?" (John 20:13). She thought that the Lord was the gardener and asked if he had taken the body of Jesus and if he had if he would tell her where he had laid Him so she could take Him away. Jesus called her by name, and she turned to Him and recognized Him and called Him "Rabboni; which is to say, Master" (John 20:16). She must have reached toward Him because Jesus told her, "Touch me not; for I am not yet ascended to my Father: but go to my brethren, and say unto them, I ascend unto my Father, and your Father; and to my God, and your God" (verse 17). Mary did as He requested and went and told the disciples that she had seen the Lord and that He had spoken those things to her.

MARK 16:9–11

9 Now when Jesus was risen early the first day of the week, he appeared first to Mary Magdalene, out of whom he had cast seven devils.

10 And she went and told them that had been with him, as they mourned and wept.

11 And they, when they had heard that he was alive, and had been seen of her, believed not.

JOHN 20:11–18

11 But Mary stood without at the sepulchre weeping: and as she wept, she stooped down, and looked into the sepulchre,

12 And seeth two angels in white sitting, the one at the head, and the other at the feet, where the body of Jesus had lain.

13 And they say unto her, [Two Angels] **Woman, why weepest thou? She saith unto them, Because they have taken away my Lord, and I know not where they have laid him.**

14 And when she had thus said, she turned herself back, and saw Jesus standing, and knew not that it was Jesus.

15 Jesus saith unto her, [Jesus] **Woman, why weepest thou? whom seekest thou?** She, supposing him to be the gardener, saith unto him, [Mary Magdalene] **Sir, if thou have borne him hence, tell me where thou hast laid him, and I will take him away.**

16 Jesus saith unto her, [Jesus] **Mary.** She turned herself, and saith unto him, [Mary] **Rabboni;** which is to say, Master.

17 Jesus saith unto her, [Jesus] **Touch me not; for I am not yet ascended to my Father: but go to my brethren, and say unto them, I ascend unto my Father, and your Father; and to my God, and your God.**

18 Mary Magdalene came and told the disciples that she had seen the Lord, and that he had spoken these things unto her.

90

JESUS APPEARS TO OTHER WOMEN

MATTHEW 28:9–10
Location: Near Jerusalem

Summary

After the encounter with Mary Magdalene, Jesus must have ascended to the Father and then returned to greet other women who held Him by the feet and worshipped Him. He invited them not to be afraid but to go tell His brethren to go into Galilee and there they would see Him.

MATTHEW 28:9–10

9 And as they went to tell his disciples, behold, Jesus met them, saying, [**Jesus**] **All hail.** And they came and held him by the feet, and worshipped him.

10 Then said Jesus unto them, [**Jesus**] **Be not afraid: go tell my brethren that they go into Galilee, and there shall they see me.**

91

OTHERS RESURRECTED AND APPEAR UNTO MANY

MATTHEW 27:52–53
Location: Near Jerusalem

Summary

After the resurrection of the Lord, others were also resurrected and were able to appear to loved ones.

MATTHEW 27:52–53

52 And the graves were opened; and many bodies of the saints which slept arose,

53 And came out of the graves after his resurrection, and went into the holy city, and appeared unto many.

92

OFFICIALS BRIBE SOLDIERS

MATTHEW 28:11–15
Location: Near Jerusalem

Summary

The soldiers or centurions who were guarding the sepulcher were no doubt shaken by what they had experienced. It is not clear exactly what they saw and heard, but it must have been clear to them that what had transpired was not of this earth. Therefore, they went into the city and told the chief priests who had arranged for them to watch the sepulcher. The chief priests conspired together to bribe the soldiers so that when asked they would say that Jesus' disciples had come during the night and had stolen His body. This exchange in and of itself is extraordinary. Amazingly, the chief priests continued to be hard-hearted. Even the testimony of the soldiers didn't cause them to pause and reconsider what they had done.

MATTHEW 28:11–15

11 Now when they were going, behold, some of the watch came into the city, and shewed unto the chief priests all the things that were done.

12 And when they were assembled with the elders, and had taken counsel, they gave large money unto the soldiers,

221

13 Saying, [Chief Priests] Say ye, His disciples came by night, and stole him away while we slept.

14 And if this come to the governor's ears, we will persuade him, and secure you.

15 So they took the money, and did as they were taught: and this saying is commonly reported among the Jews until this day.

93

JESUS APPEARS TO TWO DISCIPLES

MARK 16:12–13; LUKE 24:13–35
Location: Emmaus

Summary

Two of the Lord's disciples were traveling to Emmaus from Jerusalem. Earlier that morning, they had been with some of the other disciples and had found the empty tomb. While they were walking and talking about the sad events that had transpired over the last several days, the Lord drew up to them, but their eyes were "holden" that they knew Him not. The Lord asked them why they were sad. The one who was named Cleopas was surprised that the stranger wasn't aware of all the things that had transpired over the last few days in Jerusalem, so he rehearsed unto Him what had gone on. At this the Lord, referring to the chief priests, said, "O fools, and slow of heart to believe all that the prophets have spoken: Ought not Christ to have suffered these things, and to enter into his glory?" (Luke 24:25). Then the Lord began at the time of Moses and expounded all the scriptures concerning Himself.

As they approached the village in the evening, the Lord acted as if He was going to keep walking. However, they told Him that the day had been long and invited Him to stay with them that evening and to join them for dinner. He accepted the invitation and "as he sat at meat with them, he took bread, and blessed it, and brake, and gave to them. And their eyes were opened, and they knew him; and he vanished out of their sight. And they said one to another, Did not our heart burn within us, while he talked with us by the way, and while he opened to us the scriptures? And they rose up the same hour, and returned to Jerusalem, and found the eleven gathered together, and them that were with them, Saying, The Lord is risen indeed, and hath appeared to Simon. And they told what things were done in the way, and how he was known of them in breaking of bread" (verses 30–35).

MARK 16:12–13

12 After that he appeared in another form unto two of them, as they walked, and went into the country.

13 And they went and told it unto the residue: neither believed they them.

LUKE 24:13–35

13 And, behold, two of them went that same day to a village called Emmaus, which was from Jerusalem about threescore furlongs.

14 And they talked together of all these things which had happened.

15 And it came to pass, that, while they communed together and reasoned, Jesus himself drew near, and went with them.

16 But their eyes were holden that they should not know him.

17 And he said unto them, [**Jesus**] **What manner of communications are these that ye have one to another, as ye walk, and are sad?**

18 And the one of them, whose name was Cleopas, answering said unto him, [**Cleopas**] **Art thou only a stranger in Jerusalem, and hast not known the things which are come to pass there in these days?**

19 And he said unto them, [**Jesus**] **What things?** And they said unto him, [**Two men of Emmaus**] **Concerning Jesus of Nazareth, which was a prophet mighty in deed and word before God and all the people:**

20 **And how the chief priests and our rulers delivered him to be condemned to death, and have crucified him.**

21 But we trusted that it had been he which should have redeemed Israel: and beside all this, to day is the third day since these things were done.

22 Yea, and certain women also of our company made us astonished, which were early at the sepulchre;

23 And when they found not his body, they came, saying, that they had also seen a vision of angels, which said that he was alive.

24 And certain of them which were with us went to the sepulchre, and found it even so as the women had said: but him they saw not.

25 Then he said unto them, [Jesus] O fools, and slow of heart to believe all that the prophets have spoken:

26 Ought not Christ to have suffered these things, and to enter into his glory?

27 And beginning at Moses and all the prophets, he expounded unto them in all the scriptures the things concerning himself.

28 And they drew nigh unto the village, whither they went: and he made as though he would have gone further.

29 But they constrained him, saying, [Two men of Emmaus] Abide with us: for it is toward evening, and the day is far spent. And he went in to tarry with them.

30 And it came to pass, as he sat at meat with them, he took bread, and blessed it, and brake, and gave to them.

31 And their eyes were opened, and they knew him; and he vanished out of their sight.

32 And they said one to another, [Two men of Emmaus] Did not our heart burn within us, while he talked with us by the way, and while he opened to us the scriptures?

33 And they rose up the same hour, and returned to Jerusalem, and found the eleven gathered together, and them that were with them,

34 Saying, [Two men of Emmaus] The Lord is risen indeed, and hath appeared to Simon.

35 And they told what things were done in the way, and how he was known of them in breaking of bread.

94

EVENING: JESUS APPEARS TO DISCIPLES

MARK 16:14; LUKE 24:36–49; JOHN 20:19–23
Location: Jerusalem

Summary

After He appeared to the disciples on the road to Emmaus, Jesus appeared to His eleven Apostles (except Thomas), who were together in a closed room because they feared the Jews.

Mark's account said that the Lord "upbraided them" because they did not believe those who had seen Him after He had risen, suggesting that the Lord was disappointed in them because they did not have faith in His teachings that He would rise the third day, nor did they have faith in their fellow servants who had already seen Him.

The Lord then said, "Peace be unto you" (Luke 24L36), but they were frightened by this. He said to them, "Why are ye troubled? and why do thoughts arise in your hearts? Behold my hands and my feet, that it is I myself: handle me, and see; for a spirit hath not flesh and bones, as ye see me have" (verses 38–39). Then He showed them His hands and feet. He also asked them for some broiled fish and honeycomb, which He took and ate before them. Afterward, He taught them the scriptures regarding the law of Moses and how all things would be fulfilled and how He would rise from the dead the third day.

He also spoke to them about the preaching of repentance and the remission of sins to all the world beginning at Jerusalem and that they were special witnesses of His life and resurrection. He told them that before they go out into all the world they should first wait in Jerusalem until they were "endued with power from on high" (verse 49) as promised from the Father. He bestowed the Holy Ghost on them and told them that "whosoever sins ye remit, they are remitted unto them; and whose so ever sins ye retain, they are retained" (John 20:23).

MARK 16:14

14 Afterward he appeared unto the eleven as they sat at meat, and upbraided them with their unbelief and hardness of heart, because they believed not them which had seen him after he was risen.

LUKE 24:36–49

36 And as they thus spake, Jesus himself stood in the midst of them, and saith unto them, [Jesus] **Peace be unto you.**

37 But they were terrified and affrighted, and supposed that they had seen a spirit.

38 And he said unto them, [Jesus] **Why are ye troubled? and why do thoughts arise in your hearts?**

39 Behold my hands and my feet, that it is I myself: handle me, and see; for a spirit hath not flesh and bones, as ye see me have.

40 And when he had thus spoken, he shewed them his hands and his feet.

41 And while they yet believed not for joy, and wondered, he said unto them, [Jesus] **Have ye here any meat?**

42 And they gave him a piece of a broiled fish, and of an honeycomb.

43 And he took it, and did eat before them.

44 And he said unto them, [Jesus] **These are the words which I spake unto you, while I was yet with you, that all things must be fulfilled, which were written in the law of Moses, and in the prophets, and in the psalms, concerning me.**

45 Then opened he their understanding, that they might understand the scriptures,

46 And said unto them, [Jesus] Thus it is written, and thus it behoved Christ to suffer, and to rise from the dead the third day:

47 And that repentance and remission of sins should be preached in his name among all nations, beginning at Jerusalem.

48 And ye are witnesses of these things.

49 And, behold, I send the promise of my Father upon you: but tarry ye in the city of Jerusalem, until ye be endued with power from on high.

JOHN 20:19–23

19 Then the same day at evening, being the first day of the week, when the doors were shut where the disciples were assembled for fear of the Jews, came Jesus and stood in the midst, and saith unto them, [Jesus] Peace be unto you.

20 And when he had so said, he shewed unto them his hands and his side. Then were the disciples glad, when they saw the Lord.

21 Then said Jesus to them again, [Jesus] Peace be unto you: as my Father hath sent me, even so send I you.

22 And when he had said this, he breathed on them, and saith unto them, [Jesus] Receive ye the Holy Ghost:

23 Whosoever sins ye remit, they are remitted unto them; and whose so ever sins ye retain, they are retained.

95

THOMAS ABSENT, DOES NOT BELIEVE

JOHN 20:24–25
Location: Jerusalem

Summary

For some reason, the Apostle Thomas was not with the others when the Lord appeared to them. When they told him about the Lord's appearance, he did not believe. He said that he would not believe until he felt the print of the nails and thrust his hand into His side.

JOHN 20:24–25

24 But Thomas, one of the twelve, called Didymus, was not with them when Jesus came.

25 The other disciples therefore said unto him, We have seen the Lord. But he said unto them, [**Thomas**] **Except I shall see in his hands the print of the nails, and put my finger into the print of the nails, and thrust my hand into his side, I will not believe.**

96

EIGHT DAYS LATER WITH THOMAS

JOHN 20:26–29
Location: Jerusalem

Summary

The Apostle Thomas was not in attendance when the Lord showed Himself to His disciples, and he did not believe his fellow brethren when they told him they had seen the Lord. Eight days after this event when they were together again, the Savior appeared to them and said, "Peace be unto you" (John 20:26). He then invited Thomas to behold His hands and to thrust his hand into His side that he may know that the Lord lives. The Lord also invited Thomas not to be faithless but be believing. Thomas exclaimed, "My Lord and my God" (John 20:28). The Lord then taught that blessed are those that have not seen but have yet believed.

JOHN 20:26–29

26 And after eight days again his disciples were within, and Thomas with them: then came Jesus, the doors being shut, and stood in the midst, and said, [**Jesus**] **Peace be unto you.**

27 Then saith he to Thomas, [**Jesus**] **Reach hither thy finger, and behold my hands; and reach hither thy**

hand, and thrust it into my side: and be not faithless, but believing.

28 And Thomas answered and said unto him, [Thomas] My Lord and my God.

29 Jesus saith unto him, [Jesus] Thomas, because thou hast seen me, thou hast believed: blessed are they that have not seen, and yet have believed.

97

PURPOSE OF JOHN'S GOSPEL

JOHN 20:30–31
Location: Unknown

Summary

John points out that his gospel account does not include all the signs that Jesus did in the presence of His disciples. The signs he did include are there to encourage us to believe that Jesus is the Christ, the Son of God, and that as we seek the Lord we "might have life through his name" (John 20:31).

JOHN 20:30–31

30 And many other signs truly did Jesus in the presence of his disciples, which are not written in this book:

31 But these are written, that ye might believe that Jesus is the Christ, the Son of God; and that believing ye might have life through his name.

98

PETER: "I GO FISHING"

JOHN 21:1–19
Location: Galilee

Summary

After the Lord had shown Himself to His disciples a second time, Peter and some of his brethren said that they were going to go fishing, which suggests that in the absence of clear direction they reverted to what they had done before the Lord called them the first time. They had fished from a boat most of the night and had not caught anything. They must have been close to the shore of Tiberias because they heard someone from the shore say, "Children, have ye any meat" (John 21:5)? They answered no but did not recognize that it was the Lord. The Lord told them that if they cast their net on the right side of the ship, they would catch fish. When they did as the stranger had directed, the nets became so full of fish that they were unable to draw them in. John the Beloved said to Peter, "It is the Lord" (verse 7). Peter jumped into the sea to swim to the Lord. The other disciples brought the ship to shore as they dragged the nets full of 153 fishes.

When the disciples came ashore, they found a fire of coals and fish ready to eat, as well as bread. It appears that they were a little apprehensive about approaching the Lord and calling Him by name, so He took some fish and bread and gave them to eat and invited them to dine with Him. The scripture notes that this was the third time that He had shown Himself to them since He had risen from the dead.

During or after they had eaten, the Lord said to Peter, "Simon, son of Jonas, lovest thou me more than these? He saith unto him, Yea, Lord; thou knowest that I love thee. He saith unto him, Feed my lambs. He saith to him again the second time, Simon, son of Jonas, lovest thou me? He saith unto him, Yea Lord; thou knowest that I love thee. He saith unto him, Feed my sheep. He saith unto him the third time, Simon, son of Jonas, lovest thou me? Peter was grieved because he said unto him the third time, Lovest thou me? And he said unto him, Lord, thou knowest all things; thou knowest that I love thee. Jesus saith unto him, Feed my sheep (John 21:15–17). After this interaction with Peter, the Lord said to him, "Follow Me." Before this invitation from Jesus, Peter was adrift and uncertain what to do next. With this experience, clarity came. Perhaps we are uncertain at times of what we should do next. The same invitation applies to us: "Follow me."

JOHN 21:1–19

1 After these things Jesus shewed himself again to the disciples at the sea of Tiberias; and on this wise shewed he himself.

2 There were together Simon Peter, and Thomas called Didymus, and Nathanael of Cana in Galilee, and the sons of Zebedee, and two other of his disciples.

3 Simon Peter saith unto them, [Peter] I go a fishing. They say unto him, [Apostles] **We also go with thee. They went forth, and entered into a ship immediately; and that night they caught nothing.**

4 But when the morning was now come, Jesus stood on the shore: but the disciples knew not that it was Jesus.

5 Then Jesus saith unto them, [Jesus] **Children, have ye any meat?** They answered him, [Apostles] **No.**

6 And he said unto them, [Jesus] **Cast the net on the right side of the ship, and ye shall find. They cast therefore, and now they were not able to draw it for the multitude of fishes.**

7 Therefore that disciple whom Jesus loved saith unto Peter, [John the Beloved] **It is the Lord. Now when Simon Peter heard that it was the Lord, he girt his fisher's coat unto him, (for he was naked,) and did cast himself into the sea.**

8 And the other disciples came in a little ship; (for they were not far from land, but as it were two hundred cubits,) dragging the net with fishes.

9 As soon then as they were come to land, they saw a fire of coals there, and fish laid thereon, and bread.

10 Jesus saith unto them, [Jesus] **Bring of the fish which ye have now caught.**

11 Simon Peter went up, and drew the net to land full of great fishes, an hundred and fifty and three: and for all there were so many, yet was not the net broken.

12 Jesus saith unto them, [Jesus] **Come and dine. And none of the disciples durst ask him, Who art thou? knowing that it was the Lord.**

13 Jesus then cometh, and taketh bread, and giveth them, and fish likewise.

14 This is now the third time that Jesus shewed himself to his disciples, after that he was risen from the dead.

15 So when they had dined, Jesus saith to Simon Peter, [Jesus] **Simon, son of Jonas, lovest thou me more than these?** He saith unto him, [Peter] **Yea, Lord; thou knowest that I love thee.** He saith unto him, [Jesus] **Feed my lambs.**

16 He saith to him again the second time, [Peter] **Simon, son of Jonas, lovest thou me?** He saith unto him, [Peter] **Yea, Lord; thou knowest that I love thee.** He saith unto him, [Peter] **Feed my sheep.**

17 He saith unto him the third time, [Jesus] **Simon, son of Jonas, lovest thou me?** Peter was grieved because he said unto him the third time, Lovest thou me? And he said unto him, [Peter] **Lord, thou knowest all things; thou knowest that I love thee.** Jesus saith unto him, [Jesus] **Feed my sheep.**

18 **Verily, verily, I say unto thee, When thou wast young, thou girdedst thyself, and walkedst whither thou wouldest: but when thou shalt be old, thou shalt stretch forth thy hands, and another shall gird thee, and carry thee whither thou wouldest not.**

19 This spake he, signifying by what death he should glorify God. And when he had spoken this, he saith unto him, [Jesus] **Follow me.**

99

PETER INQUIRES ABOUT JOHN

JOHN 21:20–22
Location: Galilee

Summary

After the Lord invited Peter to follow Him, Peter asked the Lord about John: "What shall this man do" (John 21:21)? Jesus asked the question, "If I will that he tarry till I come, what is that to thee? Follow thou me" (John 21:22). This suggests that John was to tarry on the earth until the Savior returns. It is not clear if this came at a request from John or if the Lord wanted him to remain on the earth until His return. What is clear is that the Lord wants us to mind our own business and focus on the calling that He has given us at the time.

JOHN 21:20–22

20 Then Peter, turning about, seeth the disciple whom Jesus loved following; which also leaned on his breast at supper, and said, Lord, which is he that betrayeth thee?

21 Peter seeing him saith to Jesus, **[Peter] Lord, and what shall this man do?**

22 Jesus saith unto him, **[Jesus] If I will that he tarry till I come, what is that to thee? follow thou me.**

100

TESTIMONY ABOUT JOHN

JOHN 21:23–25; 3 NEPHI 28:6;
DOCTRINE & COVENANTS 7
Location: Unknown

Summary

John, the author of this Gospel, suggests it was known among the brethren that he would not die but would tarry on the earth until the Savior returns. It is not clear in these verses if John had asked the Savior if he could remain on the earth until He comes again or if that is what the Lord wanted him to do. However, it is clear from the Book of Mormon and the Doctrine and Covenants that it was John who made the request that he may tarry on the earth and bring souls unto Christ.

John testifies that his writings about the life of Christ are true and then concludes his gospel by pointing out that his writings are just a small fraction of all that could be written about the Savior.

JOHN 21:23–25

23 Then went this saying abroad among the brethren, that that disciple should not die: yet Jesus said not unto him, He shall not die; but, If I will that he tarry till I come, what is that to thee?

24 This is the disciple which testifieth of these things, and wrote these things: and we know that his testimony is true.

237

25 And there are also many other things which Jesus did, the which, if they should be written every one, I suppose that even the world itself could not contain the books that should be written. Amen.

3 NEPHI 28:6

6 And he said unto them: [Jesus] Behold, I know your thoughts, and ye have desired the thing which John, my beloved, who was with me in my ministry, before that I was lifted up by the Jews, desired of me.

DOCTRINE AND COVENANTS 7

1 And the Lord said unto me: [Jesus] John, my beloved, what desirest thou? For if you shall ask what you will, it shall be granted unto you.

2 And I said unto him: [John] Lord, give unto me power over death, that I may live and bring souls unto thee.

3 And the Lord said unto me: [Jesus] Verily, verily, I say unto thee, because thou desirest this thou shalt tarry until I come in my glory, and shalt prophesy before nations, kindreds, tongues and people.

4 [John] And for this cause the Lord said unto Peter: [Jesus] If I will that he tarry till I come, what is that to thee? For he desired of me that he might bring souls unto me, but thou desiredst that thou mightest speedily come unto me in my kingdom.

5 I say unto thee, Peter, this was a good desire; but my beloved has desired that he might do more, or a greater work yet among men than what he has before done.

6 Yea, he has undertaken a greater work; therefore I will make him as flaming fire and a ministering angel; he shall minister for those who shall be heirs of salvation who dwell on the earth.

7 And I will make thee to minister for him and for thy brother James; and unto you three I will give this power and the keys of this ministry until I come.

8 Verily I say unto you, ye shall both have according to your desires, for ye both joy in that which ye have desired.

101

THE GREAT COMMISSION
TO THE TWELVE

MATTHEW 28:16–20; MARK 16:15–18;
MORMON 9:22–24
Location: Galilee

Summary

The Savior asked the eleven Apostles to go up to a mountain that He had specified. There He met them and told them that He had all power in heaven and earth. Then He charged them to go into all the world and preach the gospel to all nations and to baptize them in the name of the Father and of the Son and of the Holy Ghost. He also charged them with teaching all the things that He had taught and commanded them. Then He reassured them that He would always be with them and said that they would perform many miracles in His name.

MATTHEW 28:16–20

16 Then the eleven disciples went away into Galilee, into a mountain where Jesus had appointed them.

17 And when they saw him, they worshipped him: but some doubted.

18 And Jesus came and spake unto them, saying, [Jesus] All power is given unto me in heaven and in earth.

19 Go ye therefore, and teach all nations, baptizing them in the name of the Father, and of the Son, and of the Holy Ghost:

20 Teaching them to observe all things whatsoever I have commanded you: and, lo, I am with you alway, even unto the end of the world. Amen.

MARK 16:15–18

15 And he said unto them, [Jesus] Go ye into all the world, and preach the gospel to every creature.

16 He that believeth and is baptized shall be saved; but he that believeth not shall be damned.

17 And these signs shall follow them that believe; In my name shall they cast out devils; they shall speak with new tongues;

18 They shall take up serpents; and if they drink any deadly thing, it shall not hurt them; they shall lay hands on the sick, and they shall recover.

MORMON 9:22–24

22 For behold, thus said Jesus Christ, the Son of God, unto his disciples who should tarry, yea, and also to all his disciples, in the hearing of the multitude: [Jesus] Go ye into all the world, and preach the gospel to every creature;

23 And he that believeth and is baptized shall be saved, but he that believeth not shall be damned;

24 And these signs shall follow them that believe— in my name shall they cast out devils; they shall speak with new tongues; they shall take up serpents; and if they drink any deadly thing it shall not hurt them; they shall lay hands on the sick and they shall recover.

102

ASCENSION, PROCLAMATION

MARK 16:19–20; LUKE 24:50–53
Location: Near Jerusalem

Summary

After the Lord taught His Apostles on the mountain, He blessed them and then "ascended into heaven, to sit down on the right hand of the Father, to reign with almighty power according to the will of the Father" (D&C 20:24.) Paul picks up from the Gospel writers and gives us more insight into the ascension by noting that "while they looked steadfastly toward heaven as he went up, behold, two men stood by them in white apparel; which also said, Ye men of Galilee, why stand ye gazing up into heaven? This same Jesus, which is taken up from you into heaven shall so come in like manner as ye have seen him go into heaven. Then returned they unto Jerusalem from the mount called Olivet, which is from Jerusalem a sabbath day's journey" (Acts 1:11).

Both Mark and Luke end their gospel messages by giving us some insight into what the Apostles did after the ascension. Luke said they were continually in the temple praising and blessing God. Mark said they went forth and preached everywhere and the Lord was working with them.

Combined, these two gospel authors provide us a pattern of how we are to prepare to serve the Lord—spending time in the temple preparing ourselves spiritually to receive direction from the Holy Ghost, and going forth to serve as we have been directed, all the while knowing that the Lord is working with us.

MARK 16:19–20

19 So then after the Lord had spoken unto them, he was received up into heaven, and sat on the right hand of God.

20 And they went forth, and preached every where, the Lord working with them, and confirming the word with signs following. Amen.

LUKE 24:50–53

50 And he led them out as far as to Bethany, and he lifted up his hands, and blessed them.

51 And it came to pass, while he blessed them, he was parted from them, and carried up into heaven.

52 And they worshipped him, and returned to Jerusalem with great joy:

53 And were continually in the temple, praising and blessing God. Amen.

CONCLUSION

As I conclude this study, I can't help but walk back in time and think about some of the seminal events of the Savior's last week on earth. I think about the Lord joining His friends for dinner and Mary pouring spikenard from an alabaster box onto His head and feet and then wiping His feet with her hair; about His triumphal entry into Jerusalem and the Lord's pronouncement to the Pharisees that if the people didn't shout Hosanna to His name that the very stones would do so; about the cleansing of the temple and His declaration that "My house shall be called the house of prayer; but ye have made it a den of thieves"; I think about His many powerful parables and teachings, including the widow's mite, the ten virgins, the talents, and the sheep and goats.

I think about the Last Supper and the washing of His Apostle's feet, excusing Judas and instituting the sacrament; about the intercessory prayer and then the departure to the Mount of Olives and the Garden of Gethsemane; about His invitation to eight of His Apostles to "Sit ye here, while I go pray yonder"; about Him taking Peter, James, and John a little farther into the Garden and asking them to "watch" with Him; about Him going about a stone's throw and falling on His face and praying, "Oh my Father, if it be possible, let this cup pass from me: nevertheless not as I will, but as thou wilt."

I think about the night in agony as He took upon Him the sins of the world; about the great drops of blood He sweat, for you and for me; about His invitation to His disciples to awake for His betrayer was approaching; about Judas planting the betrayer's kiss and Peter's enthusiasm to defend the Lord with the sword; about the Lord healing the servant's ear and teaching Peter that if He wanted, He could call down twelve legions of angels.

I think about Jesus being arrested and the disciples fleeing; about His hearings before the Chief Priests, Caiaphas, Pilate, Herod, and then back to Pilate; about Pilate's capitulation and a murderer released; about Jesus scourged and mocked and then taken to Golgotha; about the crucifixion of our Lord by the soldiers and the casting of lots for His garments; about the people gathering to watch His suffering and His tenderness toward His mother; about the gathering darkness and His complete submission to His Father and His announcement that it was finished.

I think about His death, the earthquake, and the veil of the temple being rent; about the approaching Sabbath and His side pierced by a spear; about the courageous friends who retrieved His body, prepared it for burial, and placed it in the sepulcher.

I think about the Chief Priests and Pharisees sealing the tomb, the centurion watching guard over the tomb; about the angel descending from heaven and rolling back the stone; about the women finding the open tomb and the angels declaring, "He is Risen!" and then hurrying to tell the Apostles; about Peter and John running back to the tomb to find it empty.

I think of the Lord appearing to Mary Magdalene and inviting her to "touch me not for I am not yet ascended to my Father"; of the Savior's walk with two disciples on the road to Emmaus; of Jesus appearing to His disciples while Thomas was absent, and of a later occasion when Jesus invited Thomas to "reach hither thy finger, and behold my hands; and reach hither thy hand, and thrust it into my side."

I think about the Apostles, in a period of uncertainty, going fishing; about the invitation from Jesus to cast their nets on the other side, and they were filled; about Peter jumping into the water and swimming to the Lord.

I think about the Lord's invitation to Peter to feed His sheep; about the Savior with His Apostles on a mountain where He taught them and charged them to go into all the world and preach His gospel to all nations; about His ascension to sit down on the right hand of His Father; about His appearance to a fourteen-year-old boy in upstate New York to usher in the dispensation of the fulness of times. And last of all, I think about His second coming where "every knee shall bow and every tongue confess" that Jesus is the Christ.

I'm humbled by the tender experiences I have had while working on this manuscript. Even though I have never been to the Holy Land, I feel as if I have walked where Jesus walked, heard what Jesus said, and saw what Jesus experienced. I have felt a full range of emotions and found my eyes filled with tears one minute and my heart overflowing for joy the next. I'm in awe of the Savior's attributes, and I love Him dearly.

As I reflect upon my mortal weaknesses, I'm so grateful for the Savior's Atonement and the opportunity to be cleansed, healed, and comforted so that I may return to live with Him someday. I'm grateful for the Gift of the Holy Ghost and the tender witness He provides me of the truthfulness of the Savior's life and divine mission. I'm grateful for the restored gospel of Jesus Christ on the earth today and of a living prophet that guides me.

In the name of Jesus Christ, Amen.

ENDNOTES

1. The New Testament as published by The Church of Jesus Christ of Latter-day Saints (2013). Harmony of the Gospels, Section IV, The Last Week: Atonement and Resurrection, 769.

2. "The Feast of the Passover was instituted to commemorate the passing over the houses of the children of Israel in Egypt when God smote the firstborn of the Egyptians, and more generally the redemption from Egypt (Ex. 12:27; 13:15). The first Passover differed somewhat from those succeeding it. On the 10th Abib (March or April) a male lamb (or kid) of the first year, without blemish, was chosen for each family or two small families in Israel. It was slain by the whole congregation between the evenings (between sunset and total darkness) of the 14th Abib, and its blood sprinkled on the lintel and two sideposts of the doors of the houses. It was roasted with fire, and no bone of it was broken. It was eaten standing, ready for a journey, and in haste, with unleavened loaves and bitter herbs. Anything left was burned with fire, and no persons went out of their houses until the morning" (Bible Dictionary, "Feasts").

3. Jerusalem: "Formerly Salem (Gen. 14:18; Ps. 76:2), a Jebusite city until it was captured by David (2 Sam. 5:6–9); for its earlier history see Josh. 10:1–5, 23; 12:10; 15:8; 18:16, 28; Judg. 1:7–8; 19:10; 1 Sam. 17:54. It lay on the frontier line between Judah and Benjamin and was chosen by David to be his capital. Until then it had been merely a mountain fortress, about 2600 feet above sea level, surrounded by deep valleys on all sides except the north. On the east was the Valley of the Kidron, dividing the Temple Mountain from the Mount of Olives; on the west and south was the Valley of Hinnom. The plateau on which the city stands was originally divided by another valley, called by Josephus the Tyropaean Valley, now in great part filled up with debris. (See map of Jerusalem in the Map Section.) All authorities agree in placing the temple on the eastern hill, but there has been much dispute as to the position of Zion. (See Zion.) David fortified the city, the chief feature in the fortifications being a tower called the Millo. It may have protected the city on the north, the only side on which it had not the defense of precipitous ravines. During David's reign the city was little more than a fortress, the king occupying a wooden palace, and the ark still dwelling "in curtains." During the reign of Solomon much was done toward beautifying the city, the chief buildings erected being the temple (see Temple of Solomon) and the king's palace, to which was given

the name of "the house of the forest of Lebanon." After the division of the kingdoms Jerusalem remained the capital of Judah. It was frequently attacked by invading armies (1 Kgs. 14:25; 2 Kgs. 14:13; 16:5; 18–19; 24:10; 25). Under Hezekiah it was made the one center of religious worship, and the "high places" were abolished. After the return it was gradually rebuilt (Ezra 1; 3; 5; Neh. 3–4; see also Temple of Zerubbabel) but was captured and partly destroyed by Ptolemy I in 320 B.C. and by Antiochus Epiphanes in 168 B.C. The city grew under the Maccabees, and during the reign of John Hyrcanus the fortress, known in later days as the Castle Antonia, was rebuilt on the temple area. It was again captured in 65 B.C. by Pompey, who forced an entrance on the Sabbath. Herod rebuilt the walls and the temple, beautifying the city at great expense, but in A.D. 70 it was entirely destroyed by the Romans under Titus. During these later years of its history the Holy City was regarded with intense affection by all Jews, and the words of one of the Psalms of the captivity, "If I forget thee, O Jerusalem, let my right hand forget her cunning" (Ps. 137:5), express a feeling that has outlasted 25 centuries of trial and 18 continuous centuries of alienation (see also Ps. 122)" (Bible Dictionary, "Jerusalem").

4. Purification: "There were various purifying ceremonies. Bathing the flesh and the clothes in running water was used in all and sufficed in the simplest cases. When the uncleanness was of a deeper character, a purifying water for sprinkling was provided: for example, after contact with a corpse, water mingled with the ashes of a red cow (Num. 19:9); for the leper, water in which the blood of a bird had been allowed to fall (Lev. 14:6). In some cases sin and trespass offerings were also made, such as for a man with an issue (Lev. 15:13–14); a woman after childbirth (Lev. 12:6, 8); and above all, the leper (Lev. 14:2–32)" (Bible Dictionary, "Purification").

5. Pharisees: "A religious party among the Jews. The name denotes separatists. They prided themselves on their strict observance of the law and on the care with which they avoided contact with things gentile. Their belief included the doctrine of immortality and resurrection of the body and the existence of angels and spirits. They upheld the authority of oral tradition as of equal value with the written law. The tendency of their teaching was to reduce religion to the observance of a multiplicity of ceremonial rules and to encourage self-sufficiency and spiritual pride. They were a major obstacle to the reception of Christ and the gospel by the Jewish people. For the Lord's judgment on them and their works see Matthew 23; Mark 7; Luke 11:37–54" (Bible Dictionary, "Pharisees").

6. Temple of Herod: "To win popularity with the Jews, Herod, in the 18th year (17 B.C.) of his reign, proposed to rebuild the temple of Zerubbabel. The Jews feared lest, having pulled down, he should be unable to rebuild, and to reassure them, Herod promised to gather materials before he began the work. The area of the temple site was inadequate for his design, and to enlarge it he built up a wall from the bottom of the valley, binding rocks together with lead and iron and filling

up the hollows. By this means he obtained a site nearly square, each side being 600 feet. The temple proper was built by the priests themselves in a year and six months. The cloisters (the specialty of Herod's temple) and outer enclosures were built in eight years. Other buildings were added from time to time. The work was proceeding all through our Lord's earthly life, and the design was not complete till the year A.D. 64, only six years before the temple's final destruction.

"The temple area was divided into courts, and the outer courts stood on the lowest ground. Ascents were made by steps successively from the court of the Gentiles to the court of the women, the courts of the men of Israel and of the priests, and the temple itself. In the midst, not in the center of the site (but somewhat to the north and west of it), on the exact site of the temple of Solomon, with its porch facing the east and its Holy of Holies to the west, was placed the temple itself. It was thus visible from every part of the city. The temple area was surrounded on all sides by a high wall. Cloisters ran all around the wall. Those on the eastern side were called Solomon's Porch and were rebuilt by Herod. The cloisters, with the open space, about 30 cubits wide, adjoining them on the inside, formed the court of the Gentiles. The court of the women comprised the easternmost portion of the inner temple. It was entered on the east by Nicanor's Gate, a gate of Corinthian brass, reckoned to be the principal gate. This is without doubt the gate 'called Beautiful' of Acts 3:2. A wall separated the more sacred portions of the temple toward the west from the court of the women. From the latter the court of the men of Israel was reached by an ascent of 15 steps. A partition one cubit high compassed the holy house and altar and kept the people from the priests. The eastern part of this enclosure was called the court of the priests, and in it stood the huge altar of burnt offering and the laver for the priestly purifications. Twelve steps led from the court of the priests to the temple itself. The temple was 100 cubits long, 100 or 120 cubits high, the center being higher than the wings; 100 cubits broad at the porch, 60 cubits behind. The Holy Place and Holy of Holies were the same size as in Solomon's or Zerubbabel's temple. In front of the temple was a remarkable gateway without doors, with lintels above, adorned with colored and embroidered curtains. It was covered with gold, and a golden vine was spread upon it. Thirty-eight little chambers in three stories surrounded the temple, 15 on the north, 15 on the south, and 8 on the west.

"The temple, like that of Zerubbabel, had no ark. A stone was set in its place, on which the high priest placed the censer on the Day of Atonement. It followed the tabernacle (not Solomon's temple) in having only one candlestick and one table of shewbread.

"Along the walls of the inner temple were placed chambers for various purposes connected with the temple services. At the north end of the court of the women stood the treasury; at its south end the Gazith, or chamber of hewn stone, in which the Sanhedrin sat. At the northwest corner of the temple, Herod erected the fortress of Antonia. From its southeast tower, 70 cubits high, the whole temple could be viewed. A Roman legion formed its garrison. Subterranean passages connected it with the temple cloisters, and through these the Roman soldiers poured down to repress the constantly occurring disturbances in the temple courts.

"Of the places above mentioned, the court of the women was the scene of the Lord's temple teachings. In the Treasury, at its northern end, He taught (John 8:20); over against the Treasury, He sat and watched the people casting in their alms (Mark 12:41). It was the court of the Gentiles that He purified from the moneychangers; and in Solomon's Porch, at its east end, He walked in the winter (John 10:22). To the same porch gathered all the people greatly wondering (Acts 3:11), after Peter and John had healed the lame beggar who sat at the Beautiful Gate (the gate between the courts of the Gentiles and the women). Inside the Chel and in the court of the women, the Jews from Asia laid hands on Paul. They dragged him down the 14 steps into the court of the Gentiles (the temple gates being shut behind), and then from the Tower of Antonia through the cloisters the chief captain of the band ran down to rescue him (Acts 21). In the court of the men of Israel at the Feast of Tabernacles the Lord watched the priest bring the water from the Pool of Siloam through the water gate and pour it upon the altar of burnt offering (John 7). The veil that was rent at Christ's Crucifixion hung between the Holy Place and the Holy of Holies. The pinnacle that was the scene of one of His temptations was perhaps the roof of one of the porches.

"In A.D. 70, on the evening of the anniversary of the destruction of the first temple, Herod's temple was taken and destroyed by the army of Titus. A temple to Jupiter Capitolinus was erected on the site by Hadrian" (Bible Dictionary, "Temple of Herod").

7. Bethany:"House of the poor. Village two miles from Jerusalem, on the southeast slope of Olivet; the home of Lazarus, Mary, and Martha (John 11:1–46; 12:1) and of Simon (Mark 14:3); the village in which our Lord stayed during Holy Week (Matthew 21:17; Mark 11:11)" (Bible Dictionary, "Bethany").

8. Lazarus:"Helped of God. (1) Of Bethany, brother of Martha and Mary (John 11:1–44; 12:1–2, 9–11); raised by Jesus from the dead. (2) Of the parable (Luke 16:19–25); the meaning of the name may have suggested its use here" (Bible Dictionary, "Lazarus").

9. Leper:"Leprosy is a terrible form of skin disease, still occuring in various parts of the world. Lepers were forbidden by the law to enter any walled city. If a stranger approached, the leper was obliged to cry 'unclean.' The disease was regarded as a living death, indicated by bare head, rent clothes, and covered lip. For the regulations concerning the treatment of lepers, see Lev. 13 and 14" (Bible Dictionary, "Leper").

10. Who was the woman with the alabaster box? John 12:2–8 indicates that the woman was Mary the sister of Lazarus and Martha (see Bible Dictionary—Mary). This same Mary sat at Jesus' feet (see Luke 10:39, 42) and sent for Jesus after the death of Lazarus (see John 11:1–45).

11. Spikenard: "Spikenard, also called nard, nardin, and muskroot, is a class of aromatic amber-colored essential oil derived from Nardostachys jatamansi, a flowering plant of the valerian family which grows in the Himalayas of Nepal, China, and India. The oil has been used over centuries as a perfume, a traditional medicine, or in religious ceremonies across a wide territory from India to Europe." (See Wikipedia, https://en.wikipedia.org/wiki/Spikenard; accessed January 28, 2020.)

12. What was an alabaster box? The dictionary provides the following definition for alabaster: "a fine-grained, translucent form of gypsum, typically white, often carved into ornaments." (See Dictionary.com, https://www.dictionary.com/browse/alabaster?s=t; accessed January 28, 2020.) Apparently, a box had been crafted out of alabaster to store the spikenard ointment.

13. How much is three hundred pence? About one year of wages for an average agricultural worker(see icogsfg.org/ge-maryb.html). This starts to provide some perspective on the monetary value of the spikenard that was poured on the Savior's head and feet that day.

14. It is clear from Mark 14:3–9 that an alabaster box contained very precious ointment that was reserved for tender and sacred occasions such as the burial of loved ones. I suspect it was common to use these ointments to mask the smell at the time of death, and represented a tenderness toward the loved one who had passed, similar to the display of flowers that we use today.

15. Who was Judas Iscariot? The Bible Dictionary says, "Iscariot, meaning 'belonging to Kerioth' (Josh. 15:25) in the tribe of Judah, one of 'the twelve,' and the only one who was not a Galilean. The passages in which he is mentioned are Matthew 10:4; 26:14; Mark 3:19; 14:10; Luke 6:16; 22:3; John 6:71; 12:4; 13:2, 26; Acts 1:16, 25" (Bible Dictionary, "Judas"). He was the one who betrayed the Savior for thirty pieces of silver and then subsequently hung himself.

16. "Just prior to the crucifixion, Christ was anointed with expensive oils. The act was criticized by Judas who suggested that the items could have been sold to benefit the poor. Christ's response was telling. He said 'for ye have the poor always with you; but me ye have not always. For in that she hath poured this ointment on my body, she did it for my burial' (Matthew 26:11–12). Just as with this event that served to the preparation for the eternal sacrifice of Christ, even so Temples serve to the eternal blessing of the rest of us and make Christ's sacrifice effective in the exaltation of God's children. The reality is that eternal salvation is the point of this earth life. Poverty, while certainly tragic and deserving of our individual sacrifices and attention, will only pertain to this existence. In the gospel, we must seek to find the appropriate balance. Temples are built for the blessings of individuals and families into the eternities. Like the anointing of Christ, their existence serves an eternal cause and are in fact considered the House of the Lord. Just as the use of the oils were deserving of the expense, Latter-day Saints likewise consider constructing temples where sacred, eternal covenants pertaining to eternal exaltation are made, are deserving of our best efforts and sacrifices. Because the ordinances of the

temple make all of the purposes of life complete and worthwhile, the temples command a level of attention like almost none other in the church." (See https://www.fairmormon.org/answers/Mormonism_and_temples/Criticisms#Question:_Why_does_the_church_spend_so_much_money_on_temples_when_children_are_dying_of_starvation.3F; accessed January 28, 2020.)

17. Who was Lazarus? "Helped of God. (1) Of Bethany, brother of Martha and Mary (John 11:1–44; 12:1–2, 9–11); raised by Jesus from the dead" (Bible Dictionary, "Lazarus").

18. Bethphage: "House of figs. A village or district near Bethany to which Jesus sent disciples to obtain a donkey on which He could ride in the triumphal entry into Jerusalem (Matthew 21:1; Mark 11:1; Luke 19:29). Its site has never been exactly determined, but it is near the Mount of Olives and the road from Jericho" (Bible Dictionary, "Bethpage").

19. The Mount of Olives or Mount Olivet is a mountain ridge east of and adjacent to Jerusalem's Old City. It is named for the olive groves that once covered its slopes. The southern part of the Mount was the Silwan necropolis, attributed to the ancient Judean kingdom. The Mount has been used as a Jewish cemetery for over 3,000 years and holds approximately 150,000 graves, making it central in the tradition of Jewish cemeteries. Several key events in the life of Jesus, as related in the Gospels, took place on the Mount of Olives, and in the Acts of the Apostles it is described as the place from which Jesus ascended to heaven. Because of its association with both Jesus and Mary, the Mount has been a site of Christian worship since ancient times and is today a major site of pilgrimage for Catholics, the Eastern Orthodox, and Protestants. (See Wikipedia, https://en.wikipedia.org/wiki/Mount_of_Olives; accessed January 28, 2020.)

20. James E. Talmage, *Jesus the Christ*, 3rd ed. [1916], 517.

21. Hosanna: "Save now. The word is taken from Ps. 118:25, one of the Psalms of the Hallel. The chanting of this psalm was connected at the Feast of Tabernacles with the waving of palm branches; hence the use of the word by the multitudes at our Lord's triumphal entry into Jerusalem (Matthew 21:9, 15; Mark 11:9–10; John 12:13)" (Bible Dictionary, "Hosanna").

22. Messiah: "An Aramaic word meaning 'the anointed.' It occurs only in Dan. 9:25–26 and John 1:41; 4:25 (Messias). Used as the title of an office, it denotes the King and Deliverer whose coming the Jews were eagerly expecting. In the New Testament the deliverer is called the Christ, which is the Greek equivalent of Messiah, and Jesus the Messiah is called Jesus the Christ, Jesus Christ, or Christ Jesus.

"Throughout the Apocrypha there is no reference to the hope of the Messiah, though during the century before the birth of Christ the hope was steadily reviving. But many Jews, as we learn from the Gospels, were looking only for a deliverer from the Roman power and for greater national prosperity; so when the Messiah came, the nation as a whole rejected Him. Only the faithful were able to see in Jesus of Nazareth the true Suffering Servant of Isa. 53, as well as the true Prophet, Priest, and King of Israel (Matthew 16:16; Luke 24:21, 26–27; John 4:25–26; Acts 3:18; 8:32–35; 17:3; 26:23)" (Bible Dictionary, "Messiah").

23. Fig tree: "Everywhere common in Palestine, both wild and cultivated. Figs were an important food. The tree is one of the earliest to show its fruitbuds, which appear before the leaves; thus a fig tree with leaves would be expected to also have fruit. Jesus' cursing the fig tree for its fruitlessness (Mark 11:12–13, 20–23) was an allusion to the fruitlessness of Israel. The time when the leaves appear indicates that summer is "nigh at hand" (Matthew 24:32–33; D&C 45:37–38; JS—M 1:38–39). For other references to figs, see Gen. 3:7; 1 Kgs. 4:25; 2 Kgs. 20:7; John 1:47–50. The sycomore, spoken of in Isa. 9:10, Amos 7:14, and Luke 19:4, was a variety of fig tree" (Bible Dictionary, "Fig tree").

24. Sadducees: "A party or caste among the Jews. The name is probably derived from Zadok, the high priest in Solomon's time. The party consisted of old high-priestly families who came to the front during the Maccabean war. They formed the Jewish aristocracy and were powerful, though quite small in numbers. In their treatment of religious questions they held to the letter of the Mosaic revelation and denied the authority of ancient tradition; they taught complete freedom of the will in moral action; they were opposed to the Pharisees as to the belief in angels and spirits; they refused also to accept the doctrine of immortality as a necessary part of the Jewish faith. It was through their influence that Greek culture spread in Israel. Their opposition to our Lord was the result of His action in cleansing the temple, which they regarded as an infringement of their rights. They opposed the work of the Apostles because they preached the Resurrection (Acts 4:1–3; 23:7–8; see also Mark 12:18–27)" (Bible Dictionary, "Sadducees").

25. Marriage: "Among the Israelites, marriage was usually preceded by a formal act of betrothal, such a contract, when once entered on, being regarded as absolutely binding. On the marriage day, the bride was escorted to her husband's home by a procession consisting of her own companions and the 'friends of the bridegroom,' or 'children of the bride-chamber,' some carrying torches and others myrtle branches and chaplets of flowers. When she reached the house, words such as 'Take her according to the law of Moses and of Israel' were spoken, the pair were crowned with garlands, and a marriage deed was signed. After the prescribed washing of hands and benediction, the marriage supper was held. For a year after marriage a man was released from all military service. The gospel law of marriage is partially given in Matthew 19:4–9; Mark 10:2–12; Rom. 7:2; 1 Cor. 7. Its meaning, as symbolizing the union between Christ and the Church, is explained in Eph. 5:22–32. Latter-day revelation tells us that marriage under the law of the gospel and the holy priesthood is for eternity and that men and women thus sealed in marriage continue to have

children throughout eternity. Although this concept of marriage is not fully presented in our present Bible, traces of it are found in Matthew 16:16–19; 19:3–8; 22:23–30; and Moses 4:18. However, the fullest explanation is found in D&C 132" (Bible Dictionary, "Marriage").

26. Resurrection: "The Resurrection consists in the uniting of a spirit body with a body of flesh and bones, never again to be divided. The Resurrection shall come to all, because of Christ's victory over death. Jesus Christ was the first to be resurrected on this earth (Matthew 27:52–54; Acts 26:23; 1 Cor. 15:23; Col. 1:18; Rev. 1:5). Others had been brought back from death but were restored to mortality (Mark 5:22–43; Luke 7:11–17; John 11:1–45), whereas a resurrection means to become immortal, with a body of flesh and bone. All will not be raised to the same glory in the Resurrection (1 Cor. 15:39–42; D&C 76), nor will all come forth at the same time (see 1 Cor. 15:23; Alma 40:8). Christ was first; the righteous have precedence over the wicked and come forth in the First Resurrection, whereas the unrepentant sinners come forth in the last resurrection (Rev. 20:5–13). The New Testament gives ample evidence that Jesus rose with His physical body: He ate fish and honey (Luke 24:42–43); He said He had flesh and bones (Luke 24:39); the people touched Him (Luke 24:39–40; John 20:25–29); the tomb was empty (Luke 24:2–3; John 20:1–10); and the angels said He had risen (Mark 16:1–6). One of the most fundamental doctrines taught by the Twelve was that Jesus was risen from the tomb, with His glorified, resurrected body, as in Acts 1:21–22; 2:32; 3:15; 4:33. To obtain a resurrection with a celestial, exalted body is the center point of hope in the gospel of Jesus Christ. The Resurrection of Jesus is the most glorious of all messages to mankind. Latter-day revelation confirms the reality of the Resurrection of Christ and of all mankind, as in Alma 11:41–45; 40; 3 Ne. 11; D&C 76; Moses 7:62" (Bible Dictionary, "Resurrection").

27. Bruce R. McConkie, *Doctrinal New Testament Commentary*, 3 vols. [1965–73], 1:606–7.

28. Scribes: "In the days of the Hebrew monarchy this was the title of a court official, a secretary of state (2 Sam. 8:17; 2 Kgs. 12:10; 18:18). After the captivity we find the title given to Ezra (7:6, 21) and to others who acted as teachers of the law. Scribes are frequently mentioned in the New Testament, being sometimes called lawyers. It was their business to develop the law in detail and apply it to the circumstances of their time; hence grew up the oral or traditional law side by side with the written law. Their method of teaching relied on memorization. Their aim was to reproduce and teach others to reproduce accurately the words of the wise (hence the office is a symbol of fidelity in instruction, Matthew 13:52). The scribes never taught on their own authority (contrast with this the Lord's method, Matthew 7:29). They taught either in houses of instruction or in the temple courts, their pupils sitting on the ground (Luke 2:46; Acts 22:3). They formed an influential part in the supreme court of the Sanhedrin. Rabbi (my Master) was the title usually given them. As a rule they were Pharisees (Mark 2:16; Acts

23:9), though there were also Sadducean scribes. In theory they received no pay for their work (but see Mark 12:38–40), and it was usual to combine the study of the law with the exercise of some other calling. Their influence considerably increased after the downfall of Jerusalem and the cessation of the temple worship. As a class they offered a determined opposition to the Lord mainly because He disregarded the "traditions of the elders" (Matthew 21:15; 26:3; Mark 8:31; 11:18; 14:1; Luke 5:30; 6:7; 9:22; 11:53; Acts 4:5; 6:12). For His opinion of them see Matthew 5:20; 15:1–9; 23:2–9; Mark 2:17; 12:38; Luke 11:44; 20:46" (Bible Dictionary, "Scribes").

29. In Matthew the discussion took place between the Lord and one of the Pharisees who was a lawyer. In Mark, the discussion took place between the Lord and one of the scribes. This suggests that scribes were essentially lawyers.

30. Bible Dictionary, "Hypocrite."

31. The lowest value coinage at the time.

32. McConkie, 78.

33. Marvin J. Ashton, "A Time of Urgency," *Ensign*, May 1974, 36.

34. *The Discourses of Wilford Woodruff*, sel. G. Homer Durham [1946], 124–25.

35. "The talent . . . was one of several ancient units of mass, a commercial weight, as well as corresponding units of value equivalent to these masses of a precious metal. The talent of gold was known to Homer, who described how Achilles gave a half-talent of gold to Antilochus as a prize.[1] A Greek, or Attic talent, was 26 kilograms (57 lb)[2] (approximately the mass of water required to fill an amphora[citation needed]), a Roman talent was 32.3 kilograms (71 lb), an Egyptian talent was 27 kilograms (60 lb),[2] and a Babylonian talent was 30.3 kilograms (67 lb).[3] Ancient Israel, and other Levantine countries, adopted the Babylonian talent, but later revised the mass.[4] The heavy common talent, used in New Testament times, was 58.9 kilograms (130 lb).[4]." (See Wikipedia, https://en.wikipedia.org/wiki/Talent_(measurement); accessed January 28, 2020.)

36. The New Testament dictionary says that this was the last day before Passover, but in the above verses it says "that after two days is the feast of the Passover."

37. Iscariot: "Iscariot, meaning 'belonging to Kerioth' (Josh. 15:25) in the tribe of Judah, one of 'the twelve,' and the only one who was not a Galilean. The passages in which he is mentioned are Matthew 10:4; 26:14; Mark 3:19; 14:10; Luke 6:16; 22:3; John 6:71; 12:4; 13:2, 26; Acts 1:16, 25" (Bible Dictionary, "Judas").

38. Talmage, 613–14.

39. Pilate: "Roman prefect in Judea, A.D. 26–36 (Luke 3:1). His headquarters were at Caesarea, but he was generally present in Jerusalem at feast time. He had a great contempt for the Jewish people and for their religion. During his term of office there was much disorder, mainly in consequence of an attempt he made to introduce into the city silver busts of the emperor on the Roman ensigns. In Luke 13:1 there is a reference to an outbreak during one of the feasts, when Pilate sent soldiers into the temple courts and certain Galileans

were slain. He is prominent in the story of our Lord's Passion (Matthew 27:2–26; 27:58–66; Mark 15:1–15, 42–47; Luke 23:1–25, 50–53; John 18:28–40; 19:1–22, 31, 38). As the Sanhedrin had no power to carry out their sentence of death, Pilate's consent had to be obtained. The Lord was therefore charged before him with stirring up sedition, making Himself a king, and forbidding to give tribute to Caesar. Pilate saw that there was no evidence to support the charge, and, having received a warning from his wife, he wished to dismiss the case. He also tried to avoid all responsibility in the matter by sending our Lord for trial to Herod Antipas, tetrarch of Galilee, but Herod sent Him back without any formal decision on the case. It was not until the Jews threatened to send a report to the Emperor Tiberius, whose suspicious nature Pilate well knew, that he passed a death sentence, knowing it to be unjust. The sentence was carried out under his directions by Roman soldiers. Pilate was removed from office a few years later in consequence of a disturbance in Samaria" (Bible Dictionary, "Pilate").

40. Talmage, chapter 35.

ABOUT THE AUTHOR

Barrett A. Slade is a professor of finance and real estate in the Marriott School of Business at Brigham Young University. He has a bachelor's degree in economics and a master's degree in managerial economics from BYU, and a Ph.D. in business from the University of Georgia. He is the author of numerous publications on real estate finance and economics.

Born and raised in Arizona, he served a mission in South Carolina before attending BYU. He has served in many callings in the Church, including Young Men president, Gospel Doctrine teacher, elders quorum president, bishop, and a member of a stake presidency.

Brother Slade and his wife, Patty, are the parents of three children and reside in Mapleton, Utah.